Quarterback
The Sale

Zach Santmier

DEDICATION

To my wife, Laur. For pushing me to dream bigger.

CONTENTS

ACKNOWLEDGMENTS

It takes a tribe. In no particular order, for your inspiration and help in writing this book: Grant Cardone - 10X pushed me to take action; Setema Gali - ManWealth changed my life; Meghan Howard – Concierge Service changed the way I view business and people; Kevin Polakovich – "I've got it"; Taylor at PaperTrue – You made this book comprehensible.

INTRO

The 15 highest-paid players in the National Football League (NFL) are all quarterbacks. Why? Simply put, they control where the ball goes on the field. When the quarterback gets in the huddle, he doesn't take a vote or give three plays he thinks might work. He leads decisively with authority and direction. His singular desired outcome is to get the ball into the end zone, and he leads the team down the field to accomplish this mission.

Running backs, wide receivers, lineman, and defensive backs are all very important, but there would be no points on the scoreboard without the leadership and direction of a quarterback directing every move. It is the quarterback who is ultimately responsible for getting the ball in the endzone and winning the game. Without that position, you don't have football. Therefore, quarterbacks are the highest-paid players on the field.

So I stepped back and asked myself: if quarterbacks are the highest-paid players in their field, how can I be the highest-paid player in my field and you in yours? This question led me down a journey of writing what you are reading today. I have found that the principles that make a valuable quarterback in football are just as true for becoming the most successful player in sales and business.

Throughout this book, you will find practices and mindsets that resonate with you. You'll find yourself saying, "Yes, I have that mindset!" or, "Yes, we do that, too!" However, the key to this book is not simply the mastery of individual skills.

We are going to dig into the Mindset of a Quarterback, the Process of a Quarterback, and the Execution by a Quarterback. Independent of one another, each section offers practical advice for leveling up your business. However, when you overlap these three components, you will find what it means to quarterback the sale, and I promise you your customers will notice the change, your sales will skyrocket, and you will feel more in control of your life.

This book is intended for the loan officer, real estate agent, financial planner, or insurance agent who is working to create distinguishable value in the marketplace. This book is intended to be read by those individuals who are looking to dominate the market. You don't toss and turn at night wondering what your competition is doing. You lose sleep over how you can create more value for your clients to the extent that it becomes inconceivable for them to do business with anyone else besides you and your company!

Most professionals stop their efforts of improvement right before they experience massive amounts of success. They don't realize that right on the other side of average are fields of green grass. They do what average people do—work at a good pace, maybe even a couple extra hours here and there. They serve their customer and treat them kindly, but don't go out of their way to bowl over their customer. What sets the successful apart from the average is their willingness to go the extra mile. In other words, what differentiates high-income earners from their average-paid counterparts is their willingness to provide extraordinary value.

Welcome to quarterbacking the sale. Quarterbacks go the extra mile, take the initiative, and go above and beyond to ensure their client gets into the endzone, and says those three magical words: "That was it?"

Becoming a quarterback is not rocket science, but it does take hard work. I've interviewed dozens of high-performing athletes and salespeople, and I've heard the same story every time: to be at your best, you must have a winning mindset, a "concierge level process", and the execution of a closer. Therefore, as you read this book, we will spend our time together on these three areas predominantly.

Chapter 1

Is There a Quarterback Inside of You?

When you bring your girlfriend home to meet your parents for the first time, it's probably best to hold ghastly football stories back until after you've married the girl. The first time I brought my now-wife, Lauren, home to meet my family in Virginia, she sat in our living room in disbelief as we recounted the story of my dad literally super gluing my friend's ear back on after it was partially torn off playing tackle football.

Growing up, I never spent Sunday afternoons on the couch. My buddies and I gathered at a local elementary school and played the sport like real men: full contact tackle football. We'd play 11 on 11 and attracted talent that went on to play Division 1 college football. Sunday afternoons were not for the faint-hearted.

Though I played only five years of organized football, I was always drawn to the position of a quarterback. However, I wasn't the most athletic person on the field, and I always felt athletically incapable of stepping into that position in organized ball. But that didn't deter me from trying to pass a ball on Sunday afternoons. Typically, Athletic Jock A would be voted to play quarterback, but I would always put my name in the hat. I liked playing the position, and when I had the opportunity, I was good at it, much to my surprise.

After college, I played in a 7 on 7 tournament, and we were getting trounced. Once again, the super athletic players were stepping up to play quarterback, but the ball was simply not moving down the field. As a last ditch effort, I decided to step up to the plate and take the quarterback position. To my surprise, we began to score. We began to march down the field and score repeatedly!

I'll be honest—I was a bit shocked at my success. When I had played ball in high school, I was a defensive end. I didn't even play offense (looking back, that was probably why I didn't enjoy playing). But as I stood to take the snap, a sense of confidence swept over me that gave me the ability to quarterback the game and lead my team to success.

I realized then that being a successful quarterback had a lot less to do with what you did (passing, running, etc.) and more to do with who you were. The quarterbacks before me could pass a ball, but they couldn't organize the team and they didn't have the vision to exploit the weaknesses in the opponent's defense. I could pass and run okay, but what I lacked in athleticism, I made up for in terms of vision and leadership.

As I've expanded my career in sales, I've noticed that the traits in top quarterbacks are also present in top performing salespeople. I was never able to play college ball or take a snap in an organized game under the lights, but I've worked hard to develop those quarterback traits and implement them into my business.

You might be able to relate. You've never been the absolute best athlete or even salesperson because you didn't believe you had the raw skill set or natural ability for it. Maybe you have believed the lie that you're not the right fit or don't deserve a shot at earning more income than you could even imagine. The only things that limit us from actualizing our fullest potential are thoughts. And then thoughts become stories we tell ourselves and believe about ourselves. Even if it's nothing more than a mental exercise, I'd like you to read the following statement out loud five times:

I am capable and worthy. I have been created for greatness. (5X)

In this book, we will discover that each of us has the capacity of becoming a quarterback in our respective fields. We will establish that this is what we were created to do as evidenced by the results of success that follow. And we will create a plan of action so you can become the quarterback you were destined to become.

My hope is that the analogy of the position of a quarterback will allow you to visualize the sales process in a fresh way. We're bombarded with the same information every single day, and for me, the most valuable information is that which allows me to view the mundane afresh. Perspective creates possibility, and I believe that by the end of this book, you will have a new perspective that will open up a world of possibilities for you.

Let's be honest: It doesn't hurt that when you become or level up to the quarterback you were created to be, you will be the highest-paid player in your field. Every single time. Guaranteed.

So what are we waiting for? Let's become quarterbacks.

ZACH SANTMIER

Part 1

Mindset of a Quarterback

When Tom Brady began his freshman year at the University of Michigan (U of M), there were 7 other quarterbacks on the depth chart. He knew earning the starting job at a highly competitive university would not be easy. Opposed to transferring to a school where he would be guaranteed some playing time, Brady determined he would stick it out and earn the starting position at U of M.

By the time he entered his sophomore year, Brady had lost 25 pounds due to appendicitis. The odds were stacked against him. He was smaller and slower than his teammates who were higher up on the roster. He didn't have any connections that could get him a starting job. All he had was determination, and he was absolutely determined to earn that coveted starting position.

At that young age, Tom Brady was wise enough to know that the starting position was not going to be won on the field or in the weight room. The starting position was going to be won in his mind first. This was good news for the young quarterback.

Greg Harden, U of M's Associate Athletic Director, began every season by meeting the entire incoming freshman athletic class. He would talk about the importance of a winning mindset and how to develop a team. Before his sophomore season, Brady walked into Harden's office, knowing that his only chance at achieving his dreams lay between his ears.

Harden took Brady under his wing and agreed to meet the young aspirant before every game. This habit would soon prove to be successful.

By the time he reached his junior year, Brady had done it. He had earned the starting position and the right to lead this Division 1 team on the field. He continued his weekly ritual before every game. Every week he would sit in Harden's office to mentally prepare for that week's game.

Tom Brady went on to win 20 out of 25 starts at U of M. His mental game had given confidence to his athleticism and he was buzzing! His success had had uncovered his NFL potential, and most people believed Brady would be a top contender in the NFL draft. His mental resilience would soon be tested again.

The day the draft arrived, teams began picking the best of the best. Early on, a quarterback was chosen, but it wasn't Brady. And then another, and another, and another. After most people had stopped watching the draft, Brady became the seventh quarterback drafted and the 199thpick overall. In the football world, this is not the position a rising star is typically drafted in. Tom Brady's mental strength was put to the test, and he would once again have to climb the ladder and earn his stripes.

Years later, Coach Bill Belichick said of Brady, "He has worked very hard on his mental understanding of the game and the process. He's earned everything he's achieved. He is not a great natural athlete...but he might go down as the best quarterback of all time." There is no doubt that Tom Brady will go down in history as one of the best if not THE best quarterbacks of all time. He has won five out of his eight Super Bowl appearances to date and continues to play at the top of his game.

So how did this 199th draft pick quarterback who didn't start until his third season at Michigan go on to become the best quarterback of all time? One word says it all: mindset.

One of the only quotes Coach Bill Belichick has displayed on the Patriots' locker room is, "Every battle is won before it is fought" (Sun Tzu *–The Art of War*). Just as in football, sales has as much to do with your mindset as it does with your skills and abilities. So as we begin this journey of becoming the quarterbacks we were created to be, we will together delve into the winning mindset of a quarterback.

Chapter 2

Grit

The foundation of every great quarterback is grit. Without grit, a quarterback's leadership, vision, determination, and control don't endure. Without grit, we could have big dreams and visions, but we wouldn't have the stamina and fortitude to see them come to fruition.

The value of successful quarterbacks is their predictability. There are many quarterbacks who can throw the ball well and run a great string of plays on a good day, but when their backs are against the wall and their coverage is blown, they don't perform at the same exceptional levels. This causes their teammates and coaches to lose faith in them and they are soon replaced with a quarterback who has what it takes to produce predictable results despite the situation. In other words, they're replaced by a quarterback who has more grit.

One of my all-time favorite quotes is by Martin Luther King Junior," If you can't run, then walk. If you can't walk, then crawl. But whatever you do, you must keep moving forward." This quote embodies grit.

I am writing this chapter following a shoulder surgery I had about three hours ago. I'm sitting in my recliner talking this book into existence because I can't type. In fact, the doctor said that I won't be able to type for the next two weeks.

So what is grit? Grit is that diesel fuel inside your gut that allows you to keep chugging along even when your circumstances are pulling you down. Grit makes you keep putting one foot in front of the other, pushing you forward to your desired destination despite what is happening around you. It is this grit that ensures you can take your client to their desired destination no matter the circumstance.

The dictionary defines grit in the sense that we're using the word—as courage, resolve, and strength of character. Deeply rooted grit gives you the ability to push through any and every obstacle that comes between you and your desire. Grit is putting one foot in front of the other, despite the cold, the incline of the hill, or the lack of feeling in your legs, as demonstrated in a later part of this chapter. Grit is HAW (hard ass work).

Grit, as the dictionary states, is courage. If you're like me, when you picture courage, you picture the lion in "Wizard of Oz." The cowardly lion never quite "had the nerve." In other words, he lacked courage. He couldn't go down the yellow brick road, because he was afraid of what might pop out at him along the way. What if a storm came? What if there were "bad guys"? Then what? The cowardly lion didn't have the courage to make it down the path until Dorothy calmed his fears and walked alongside him.

Dorothy, opposed to the cowardly lion, did have courage. This courage allowed her to lead others down a path to their desired destination—to see the Wizard of Oz. Dorothy's courage and her willingness to help others who lacked this characteristic made her the hero of the story, and she was ultimately able to help all of the friends she led.

Too many salespeople are the "cowardly lion." They lack the courage to walk down the path with their clients and help them with any and all obstacles they may encounter as they journey toward their desired destination.

It takes courage to make changes you're not necessarily comfortable with, especially when you know those changes will ensure your client gets into the end zone as seamlessly as possible.

The second part of grit is resolve. Think of men or women in your life who push through barriers no matter what. Have you ever witnessed a loved one go through a particularly trying time in their life? It could be a physical ailment or the loss of a job or intense financial stress. The men and women who go through these life altering seasons fall into one of two camps.

The first camp is self-pity. I've seen friends diagnosed with an illness and immediately go into victim mode. Statements like *"Why me?" "My life is over,"* and *"I'm ruined"* ring through the halls as they curse their condition. This is a very natural first reaction and one I am completely sympathetic toward. However, when people persist in this state for months on end, it drains them and those around them.

When folks who fall on hard times are in the second camp, everyone around them is inspired. They choose to take their condition and turn it into an opportunity to prevail. They exude a resolve to get out of whatever misfortune life has placed them in, and there is nothing that is going to stop these heroes from fighting their cursed illness. As a society, we are inspired and moved when we see this in action. There are few things more moving than someone who, against all odds, resolves in their bones that they are going to fight back and not be a victim but a victor.

Grit—Courage and Resolve. Life's struggles are afraid of men or women who exude grit, because life knows it's going to lose. Grit is the bedrock of the mental state of a predictable, winning quarterback.

When there are trials and challenges, grit pulls you through them. Grit is the bottom of your gut that tells the rest of your mind "We're not going down today!" Grit is the rock that will get you through life even when a storm comes. Grit is the rebar in concrete that tells an earthquake when it hits, "We're not going anywhere today, baby!"

The funny thing about grit is that you only know you have it when tough times come. It doesn't take grit to lay on a beach and drink pina coladas. It doesn't even take grit to close a sale or generate leads. However, it most certainly takes grit to keep trudging down the field when problems arise. I'm going to say this a million times in a million ways, but grit is the key ingredient to consistently quarterback the sale for your clients.

Quarterbacks who produce inconsistent results in the NFL get benched and lose their job soon after. The same is true for you when you quarterback the sale. When you commit to quarterbacking the sale, you are committing to produce predictable results time and time again. At the core of quarterbacking the sale are predictable and uniform results. Therefore, the most important ingredient in ensuring you have what it takes to predictably produce consistent results and quarterback the sale is, you got it, grit.

Developing Grit

So where are you at on the grit scale? When you think about dealing with problems and stepping out of your comfort zone to ensure your client's success, do you start to feel uncomfortable? A little scared? Do you welcome problem clients or run away from them? Do you pray for smooth transactions or sometimes secretly hope you'll be able to prove yourself today by solving your client's problems and trudging through the inevitably muddy waters to get them to higher, dryer ground?

I put my grit to the test in the fall of 2017 in Southern California. I attended an incredible personal development boot camp called ManWealth. Our coach, Setema Gali, brought us to the top of a hill overlooking a beautiful valley with aspirational multimillion dollar homes side-by-side. When we reached the top of the hill with 40 pound sandbags on our shoulders, Coach Setema informed us we would be marching up and down the steep slope. There was no finish line, no time limit, or no minimum number of laps we needed to complete. He just informed us that we would be marching up and down this hill in complete silence until we received further instruction. So I began to jog. There were no words of encouragement or motivation or even "at a boys."

After the first lap up and down the hill, I legitimately thought that if I made it one or two more times without passing out or collapsing, I would exceed my expectations. Coach Setema played for the New England Patriots and was on one of their winning Super Bowl teams. He knew firsthand what it took to perform at the highest level, and he was determined that day in Southern California to teach us a lesson we would never forget. He called it "low gear, no finish line." I call it grit.

As I marched up and down that hill, I had a lot of time to think in silence as the lactic acid ate away at my legs. Why in the world was I here? Why was I doing this? Who was I doing this for? And then it happened. I found my direction. I found my purpose and the answer to my deeply rooted "why."

Angela Duckworth, in her book entitled *Grit*, shares that along with courage and resolve, grit also grows the most when there is clear direction and purpose behind our actions. On that hill, I experienced this firsthand.

I realized my purpose on that hill was to lead. I believe God created me to lead others and motivate others around me to realize their truest potential. As I began running again on that hill, I started looking into the eyes of other men and encouraging them through a simple smile. I didn't shy away from my purpose, I began to embrace it.

As I embraced leading those right around me, I could hear Lauren, as if she was the 40 pound sandbag on my shoulder, kissing my ear and telling me to keep going for her and our daughters. She was encouraging me to be the most powerful serving leader I could be for her and my girls. My purpose and my direction fueled my action and propelled me to keep putting one foot in front of the other. After about 30 minutes, I was almost laughing, not because I couldn't feel my legs anymore, but because I realized that my capacity was limited only by my ability to develop grit.

Coach Setema stood with his arms crossed at the top of the hill as he watched us for 30 minutes, then 45 minutes, then an hour, and finally until nearly an hour and a half had passed. When he finally told us to line up in our boat crews, I almost didn't want to stop. I had found what I was looking for: grit. I had found the holy grail that I knew was the bedrock of every other characteristic I could develop. An entire world of possibilities had just been opened before my eyes, and I was excited to dig deep and get started.

At the top of the mountain, as we stood in rows of five, I lead our team in a sacred speech we had memorized by Theodore Roosevelt. President Roosevelt understood grit and implored the nation he was leading to exude it. This is the speech we chanted that echoed across the valleys of Southern California, a chant I know had already been recited numerous times in these multimillion dollar homes.

> *"It is not the critic who counts; not the man who points out how the strong man stumbles, or where the doer of deeds could have done them better. The credit belongs to the man who is actually in the arena, whose face is marred by dust and sweat and blood; who strives valiantly; who*

errs, who comes short again and again, because there is no effort without error and shortcoming; but who does actually strive to do the deeds; who knows great enthusiasms, the great devotions; who spends himself in a worthy cause; who at the best knows in the end the triumph of high achievement, and who at the worst, if he fails, at least fails while daring greatly, so that his place shall never be with those cold and timid souls who neither know victory nor defeat."

That is the chant of a quarterback! A true quarterback does not sit on the sidelines and point out how other people stumble. He or she is actually in the arena! Quarterbacks put the work in, strive valiantly, and err again and again! Why do they err? It is because they are always pushing themselves beyond their limits. They are always striving for improvement and doing what is required to develop grit in their lives.

So how do you develop grit? In order to develop grit, you must first seek out pain. You have to put yourself in a place where you are forced to dig into a different and deeper part of your being. It is in that deeper part of your being that grit is developed.

I developed grit on that hill. I develop grit when I make an extra ten calls in a day. This entire book has been an exercise for me in developing grit! I genuinely hope you get value and perspective out of this book, but if I'm being totally honest, the biggest reason I'm writing this book and producing a podcast is to get me **way** outside of my comfort zone. I've only written a dozen articles in my life and now here I am, typing away a book that's over a 100 pages long! I've grown more from writing this book in the past six months than perhaps in the past five years. And it's all because I'm pushing myself outside my comfort zone.

I was interviewing a top performing loan officer, and I asked him how he "proves" himself to his referral partners. I wanted to know why his referral partners referred him time and time again. His answer was perfect:

"I welcome hard files. I welcome deals that might not close. I welcome problem clients. I used to be afraid of them, but now I want them, because they give me and my team the opportunity to prove ourselves to our (real estate referral partners) agents!"

Gritty people grow to love pain. They see an obstacle in front of them as an opportunity to grow. In fact, to a gritty person, it almost becomes boring to get soft ball sales. Yes, it pays the bills and you'll always take a bigger paycheck, but do I get jacked when I close a deal without having to overcome any objections or challenges? Not really, unless it's a really big deal!

Grit is developed when we seek out and come to enjoy pain. In fact, I would argue there is no other way to develop grit. If you have a comfortable life where things come easy—where your marriage is easy, kids are perfect, and sales just glide through—my guess is that you're not growing and you're complacent. If brought to a fork in the road with two options, "Easy and pretty good life" and "Super difficult, painful, but potential massive success ahead," I predict you would pick the first option.

The Road Not Taken

Robert Frost

Two roads diverged in a yellow wood,

And sorry I could not travel both

And be one traveler, long I stood

And looked down one as far as I could

To where it bent in the undergrowth

Then took the other, as just as fair,

And having perhaps the better claim,

Because it was grassy and wanted wear;

Though as for that the passing there

Had worn them really about the same,

And both that morning equally lay

In leaves no step had trodden black.

Oh, I kept the first for another day!

Yet knowing how way leads on to way,

I doubted if I should ever come back.

I shall be telling this with a sigh,

Somewhere ages and ages hence:

Two roads diverged in a wood, and I—

I took the one less traveled by,

And that has made all the difference.

If you want to develop grit and attain massive amounts of success, we must take the road less traveled by. And which is that road less traveled by? It's the road of pain. The road less traveled is uncomfortable and always makes you dig deep. It's the road that the average joes of the world run away from, but you and I run toward, on our quest to quarterback the sale for our clients.

On the road less traveled by, we will be put to the test, challenged, and required to change in order to overcome the challenges life throws at us. Like my loan officer friend, we will begin

23

seeking out challenging files in order to prove that the process we've created will withstand even the hardest circumstances. We will be able to prove that despite all the circumstances, trials, and curveballs thrown our way, we can get every one of our clients from snap to touchdown.

David Goggins was a pest control specialist. Though he was a former Navy Seal, he had left the military and pursued a low pressure job. He would go into people's homes and spray the place to ensure little bugs weren't crawling around in any unwanted places. He had become about 100 pounds overweight, and one day, he had had enough. Goggins took action and immediately sought to push himself beyond his comfort zone.

Goggins began researching the most challenging races in the country and found a 100-mile race through the desert. Goggins called up the race director, who informed him that he couldn't run the race until he had qualified at one of their 100-mile qualifiers. It just so happened there was one more qualifying race that coming weekend. Goggins signed up for the qualifier, which was to be run around a 1-mile track. For those of you who run, running 100 miles is incredibly hard on its own, but running 100 miles around a track sounds like damnation itself. But Goggins didn't care.

Race day arrived, and David took off! His stamina surprised him as the race began, but after running in circles for half a day, Goggins began to feel the repetitive motions begin to take a toll on him. By the 70th mile, Goggins had broken every bone in his foot and had stress fractures up and down his legs. He was so physically exhausted that after sitting down for a minute at mile 70, he couldn't stand back up. His wife had to pull her limp and fatigues husband off the ground so he could finish what he started, with 30 miles to go.

To qualify, Goggins had to finish the 100 miles in less than 24 hours. This seemingly impossible task did not dissuade him. Digging deep within himself, David found the motivation to drag his sorry carcass across the finish line in just under 24 hours. This would be the first of many grueling challenges Goggins put himself through. He went on to be one of the most ultra-endurance marathoners in the world.

Goggins accomplished what he set out to do. He has shapedhimself into literally one ofthe hardest, most badass men alive. And he did this by seeking out pain—pain that most of us are unwilling to even think about.

"The pain you are willing to endure is measured by how bad you want it." - David Goggins

David Goggins was sick of being average. He was sick of not pushing himself beyond his limits and not being the best version of himself. So he took action. What action did he take? He sought out pain. Not a little pain, not even a lot of pain, but the maximum level of pain he could possibly imagine.

If you want to develop grit, you must seek out pain in all aspects of your life. Ask for harder clients, embark on physically taxing challenges, and push yourself to the limit every single day.

But don't stop there. If you want to develop grit, you must realize there is no finish line. There's never a moment in time where you've arrived. Even David Goggins, the most badass man in the world, continues to seek out pain. He pursues harder and harder challenges to continually push the limits of what he is capable of doing. You have to be OKAY with never arriving. You have to be comfortable with always being uncomfortable. You have to love the routine of pain, self-sacrifice, and pushing your limits.

Your best can always be better. I don't know where the phrase came from, but I have always had it stamped in my DNA. This is how I operate, and this is how I implore you to view your life. It should be perceived as inspirational and never demeaning. We should be excited that there are always higher peaks we can view the landscape of the world from. We should be grateful for the journey, but never sit still on the hill we've just climbed.

Your clients, referral partners, and teammates deserve the confidence that comes from your deeply developed grit. They have all placed their faith in you to get a desired result. Your clients believe that when they come to you, they will get into the end zone every single time. When your referral partners send a deal to you, they trust that you'll do what is required to make them look like a rockstar. They trust that when they send their client your way, you will ensure that despite any circumstance, their client will get into the endzone. They trust that you'll have the grit to get the job done.

If you're leading a sales team that is producing business with your name on it, your team is putting their faith in you. The loan officers, real estate agents, financial planners, and insurance agents that made it through the Great Recession from 2007 to 2009 know this first hand. I wasn't in the industry then, but I've sat down and spoken with many pros who were. The ones who made it and the few who even excelled exhibited enough grit for their team to gather around them and put their unquestioned faith in their ability to get through the hard times. It was grit that paid the bills.

So is grit important? I'd bet my life on it.

Here's where the rubber meets the road. What are you going to do about it? Will you take action, or will you nod your head and say, "Sounds good"? Will you pursue and seek out things that are painful? Will you intentionally go after challenging clients? Will you ask your referral partners to send you tougher cases so you can grow and develop grit? Will you put your body through physical pain and strain in order to develop a mindset of grit?

What action will you take today? What race will you run that will cause every bone in your foot to break? Do you have what it takes? Are you gritty enough? Do what is hard, and reap the rewards. Develop grit, and quarterback the sale.

Chapter 3

Leadership

Peyton Manning came into his rookie season as though he had been in the NFL his entire life. It didn't hurt that his dad, Archie Manning, was one of the best quarterbacks of all time, but Peyton didn't rest on his father's laurels. He knew that hard work was the only way he was going to make an impact in the NFL.

Before his first snap at training camp, Manning meticulously studied the Colts Playbook. He left no page unturned and spent all his waking hours studying play formations, play calls, and the terminologies the Colts used.

When he first got under center at training camp, he called out "Dice right, scat right, 92X." Even some of the seasoned vets didn't know that play call! But it was right out of the playbook, and what was even more impressive was that he knew how to run it. Peyton immediately got the attention of the entire team and went on to run the practice as if he had been doing so for years.

Quarterbacks are born leaders and willingly step up to the plate to assume that leadership. However, quarterbacks know that leadership and respect isn't just given, it's earned. Peyton knew there would be veterans on the team who had been in the league for years, so what did he do? He prepared. He knew that they weren't going to simply follow him because he had the title of starting quarterback. He had to earn their respect, which in turn would allow him to lead the team.

Our clients want a leader. They are imploring us to step up to the plate and lead, but they won't simply follow us if we haven't established that we know what we're talking about. What Peyton Manning did was establish this very fact. He dug deep into the playbook and, when the time was right, pulled out a play that he knew would work. His teammates agreed, and his credibility as a leader was established.

The world rewards leadership. If push comes to shove and the company's back is against the wall—I mean really against the wall—who do the employees and management turn to? They turn to the highest-paid player: the individual who exudes the most leadership and is thus the most trusted to follow.

As you continue on your journey of becoming the quarterback you were created to be, the largest indication of your success will be your level of leadership. John Maxwell, the leading authority on leadership, believes,

> *"One's leadership ability is the lid that determines his or her level of effectiveness."*

One of my favorite business stories is the McDonald's story. It is an inspiring and tragic story of leadership. The McDonald brothers had a thriving business. They had created a system that produced predictable results for their clients every time they returned to the restaurant. They had mastered a system that produced speed, quality, and consistency. When these kinds of systems are created and mastered, the natural next step for a business owner is to franchise. Typically, this is the quickest and most cost-effective way of upscaling any business, but when the McDonald brothers tried to franchise their business, it failed. Because of their failure, they thought that franchising would never be an effective business model for them, and they continued operating their original restaurant.

Then along came a man named Ray Kroc. Ray was charismatic and passionate about everything he did. He was always chasing the next big thing that could make him millions of dollars. But up until his 50s, he had achieved very little success. What he lacked in terms of monetary success, he gained in personal development. In the first 50 years of his life, Ray developed grit. He never gave up. He kept going. And as we discussed in the first chapter, his grit was the number one character trait that produced success.

It could be argued that Ray Kroc didn't fail for 50 years, it just took him 50 years to develop enough grit to achieve the monstrous amounts of success he was created for. In an exclusive deal, Ray Kroc obtained the rights from the McDonald brothers to franchise their restaurant. The rest, as they say, is history.

Grit, when developed, produces extraordinary leadership. People will follow you until kingdom come because they know you have it within you to achieve the objectives you desire.

Ray Kroc painted a vision of what the future could look like. He envisioned every American town with a cross, an American flag, and golden arches. Today, his vision has been achieved. There are towns without post offices that have a McDonald's restaurant. Ray Kroc had the grit in his gut to accomplish his vision and get the job done. This caused thousands to follow his leadership and buy into his vision.

Was Ray Kroc smarter than the McDonald brothers? Probably not. Did he work harder or for longer hours than the McDonald brothers? Perhaps at times. But what cannot be argued is that Ray Kroc exuded a higher level of leadership ability. And because of this singular fact, people bought into his vision and made this vision their own—and an American establishment was born!

When you quarterback the sale, you lead your client from snap to touchdown. As I've already said, your clients and your referral partners want to be led by you. People live in a high-pressure and high-anxiety ridden culture. And because of this, the less each person needs to have on their plate, the better. Leaders innately understand this. They cast a vision of what the future could look like, and then plot the course to achieve that desired destination. As a sales professional, just as in every other business, your level of leadership ability will be the cap of your success.

Quarterbacking the sale requires that you lead your client from snap to touchdown as quickly and as seamlessly as possible. When a quarterback gets under center, he steps into the leadership position. His team looks to him to lead them to victory.

As a sales professional, you are the quarterback, whether you like it or not. Your client is the ball, and the ball wants to be in the end zone, but the ball doesn't know what the ball doesn't know. Have you ever tried to roll a ball on the ground toward a desired location? With practice, you can roll a kickball or bowling ball precisely where you intend for it to go. Try doing that with a football. Its shape is not conducive for rolling. Footballs were created to fly through the air or be carried by another individual down the field.

Our clients are footballs. They were created to be passed and handed off. If left to their own devices, they would roll all over the field and fumble (pun intended) into the end zone. This is not because they are stupid or incapable: they simply don't do what you do for a living. They don't know every lender, home inspector, plumber, or body shop in your region. They may know one or two, but they have never had the time to find the absolute best.

As the leader of the transaction, you do have time or must create time to figure out the absolute best third party referral partners for your clients. If your client needs a plumber, lead them! Don't turn them down and say, "Good luck! Find a trusted plumber on your own!" If your client needs a lender, lead them! If you turn their request down and let them go wherever they can find the lowest rate, your client's entire home buying experience could be tarnished and, in the worst case scenario, the transaction could crumble. They want to be led, so all you and I must do is step up to the plate and lead them!

Make pointed passes and handoffs to ensure the ball advances downfield as quickly and smoothly as possible. I speak to many sales professionals who use the exact same cop out: "If I refer someone and it backfires, my client will get mad at me!" Yes, it will fall back on us. But did it backfire because our referral partner messed up, or is it because we didn't find the best referral partner in the first place?

It takes work to vet third party service professionals. We can't just refer the cards from a guy who brought donuts to our office last year. At the end of the day, we are leading the sale, and everything that happens on that field can and will fall back on us. Accept the role of a quarterback. Accept the role of a leader.

In sales, all too many professionals try to roll the ball to its desired location. They offer the client five choices and tell them to pick the one they think is best. They ask the client which direction they would like to go in to get to the end zone. Some salespeople even go as far to tell their clients that they are "low-pressure salespeople." They don't want to come across as "pushy" or "overbearing." The majority of our clients simply want the best results. In their heart of hearts, they want what is best for them, and as a professional, you have the ability to lead them to it.

This "cop out" style of leadership may get someone a handful of transactions, but no one can build a successful business and brand if they are not willing to step up to the plate and lead decisively.

Have you ever seen a quarterback get into the huddle and spend five minutes trying to gather a consensus on the best path down the field? Have you ever seen quarterbacks chatting it up with the ball and asking it the direction in which it would like to go down the field? Quarterbacks don't let the football roll down the field in any direction it wishes to go in or the direction their friends and family think it should go in. The quarterback leads decisively, making decisions and confidently declaring what he or she believes is the best path forward.

How many times do you sit the ball down on the field and abdicate your leadership role in the transaction? We will do an exercise later in the book that will help you realize when you drop the ball, but ask yourself, "When am I asking my client to do something that I can do?" or, "Do I ever shy away from leading because I'm scared of the consequences?" When we are critical of our sales process, we become prone to abdicating our leadership role in the transaction because, let's be honest, leadership and the responsibility that follows is not easy.

In my business, I refer contractors and roofers weekly. When one of my clients has shingles blown off their roof, I am the guy they call. They look to me and my team for contacts of the best roofers or contractors to help them with their problem and restore their house. Now, is that my job? No! I sold them an insurance policy. It's their job to find a contractor or a roofer. After all, if I refer a roofer and he doesn't do a good job, I could be held liable for any consequential damages. This is where most salespeople stop, but it's precisely the sort of moment where you and I can set ourselves apart from them: we quarterback, baby!

Last year, I received one of these calls, and instead of giving them the name and number of the contractor, I called Steve (not his actual name), my roofer, and asked him if he would go out, give an estimate, and repair the damages. Steve hopped on it and went out and fixed the roof, and my client was as happy as a peach, until the next windstorm came by and blew the exact same patch of roof off that was replaced.

My client didn't call Steve or the insurance company. My client, who I had convinced of Steve's abilities, called me and gave me an earful. He wasn't happy. He was pissed at Steve for doing a mediocre job and at the insurance company for saying that that's how it should have been repaired; but most of all, he was pissed at me for leading him to believe that Steve was capable of doing an exceptional job that wouldn't need to be redone. I had to figure out how to clean this mess up.

I called Steve and explained the situation to him. I wasn't happy, because at the end of the day, it was his fault that the roof had blown off despite being repaired. I don't know roofing terms, but Steve had messed something up with the fasteners that caused the roof to easily peel back a second time.

To give you some backstory, I refer between $100,000 to $150,000 worth of work to Steve every year, so we have a working relationship where he has proven himself time and time again for my clients. He had always made me look really good in front of my clients when I referred him, but this time, he had made me look like a buffoon. When you are the quarterback and you are leading the transaction, you are also in the position to hold your referral partners accountable. They are not your employees, but they are working on your behalf and at your recommendation. Your referral partners are an extension of your business, and thus, they must conduct business in a way that represents you well.

Steve had represented me well dozens of times before, and I knew he was the sort of guy who did good business. I also knew he was the sort of guy who would make things right if things went wrong. Over the phone, Steve said, "I'm really sorry about this. I'm going to go out there this afternoon and fix it. And I'm not going to charge you or your client. It was my fault, and I'm going to take care of this." I called the client back to let him know that Steve apologized for the mistake he admitted making, and he was on his way to fix it at no additional cost to my client. My client was shocked, and the eruption that occurred an hour before had been cleaned up, and my client was as happy as a peach yet again.

Leadership isn't easy, and sometimes situations get messy, but when you quarterback the sale, you will be able to lead the play confidently from snap to touchdown in such a way that your client will stand in the endzone, look back down the field and say, "Really? That was it? I thought it was going to be way worse than that!"

Developing Leadership

When preparing for this book, I read just about everything John Maxwell has written on leadership. I believe there is no other leader who is as good a teacher as John Maxwell, and I'd encourage you to begin your leadership development journey by reading two of his books: *The Leadership Handbook* and *The 21 Irrefutable Laws of Leadership*.

Though there are hundreds of excellent resources on leadership, you too have been created to lead. As a sales pro, you are already self-labeled as someone who has leadership potential at the very potential. Within you is a seed, a desire, and the raw skill to lead others. You don't need a book, a coach, or a seminar to begin leading the transaction for your client. You just need to start.

Every time you feel yourself wanting to hold back or shy away from leading the play, step forward and throw the ball. It may not be the best pass or handoff, in fact, your pass may be intercepted or fumbled. But don't be discouraged! Keep pressing forward and leading. Leaders aren't born, they are made. You will never be the perfect leader, but you can always be an evolving one.

I love what Ed Mylett always says, *"Things don't happen to you, they happen for you."* When you begin leading the play, and your passes are intercepted or your handoffs are fumbled, those turnovers didn't happen to you, they happened for you! Every dropped pass teaches you something about yourself, your process, or your referral partners. When a pass is dropped and the volcano of crap explodes on you, that didn't happen to you! It happened for you! It happened so you could learn how to be a better leader. It happened so you could improve!

Coach Setema Gali, a man I've already mentioned several times and will continue to mention, taught me a tool that has changed the way I view fumbles and interceptions. It's called the Gift. The Gift is a tool that allows everything, whether seemingly good or bad, to be viewed as positive and as a gift for your life. When leadership challenges arise, whether it's in terms of business or your personal life, ask yourself these four questions: What? Why? Lesson? Apply? Let me run my leadership incident with Steve and my client through the perspective of the Gift.

What happened? Use facts only. Don't interpret the situation or comment on it. Simply state the facts—I referred Steve to my client for a roof repair, and Steve didn't put the fasteners on correctly, which caused my client's roof to blow off a second time.

Why? Why is this a Gift? This was a Gift, because I learned that when Steve makes a mistake, he is going to make it right.

Lesson? Sometimes there are multiple lessons you can learn from a challenge. List every lesson you can think of as it applies to your situation. The more the merrier. The lesson I learned is that I need to make sure my referral partners will always make things right if they have been at fault. I need to stay calm and collected when my clients erupt and simply listen to their concerns. I need not shy away from making referrals. I just need to ensure that I always stand behind my promise and handle any situation that might arise. I could keep going, but you get the gist!

Apply? How does this situation apply to my life and my business? I now know that when I take on new referral partners, I need to ask them how they handle problems. I need to ask them for an example of a time they messed up, how they took responsibility for their mistakes, and how they made things right for their client.

You were created and born to lead. We live in a world where our client's plates are filled to the brim. They want us to lead the play and take charge. They want us to make decisive passes downfield for their benefit so when they get in the endzone, they look back down the field and say, "That was it?"

Quarterbacking starts with grit, which allows you to lead the play down the field, but you have to actually want to win. In other words, you need to have a Resolve To Win.

Chapter 4
Resolve (For the Client) to Win

Before the quarterback takes a snap, steps on the field, or even leaves the locker room, he determines success in his mind. As Tom Brady sits in the locker room before every game, he envisions winning the game. He envisions executing every play perfectly. He imagines his passes going in the hands of his intended receivers and the handoffs being smooth as his running backs take off down the field.

Top quarterbacks have a resolve to win. It's internalized and deeply rooted within them. Ben Roethlisberger can't even stand the thought of losing a ping pong match, let alone a football game. Winning is an integral part of him and every successful quarterback like him. It's not enough to simply compete. If we're not in it to win it, our clients will have no desire to enter the field with us as their quarterback.

We live in a society that "accepts" mediocrity, i.e., being middle of the pack. I was listening to the radio this morning during my drive in as the station was hosting a competition to win a TV. The DJ asked the caller a multiple choice question, and the caller got it completely wrong. Without a skip in his voice, the DJ replied, "You didn't get the right answer, but congratulations. We're still going to give you the TV for trying!" This is the world we live in. This is what we hear on our commutes and our children hear on the little league fields—*"Do you best and that's good enough."*

If this is the our modus operandi, we are going to get "squashed like the cockroaches we are," as Kevin O'Leary famously says. If we do not develop a fire within our bellies, a true resolve to win, we will not win or be the highest-paid players in our fields, and we will be trampled underfoot by our competition from every side.

When we have an insatiable desire for our clients to win, we will move a mountain with a shovel if that is what is required. My wife and I wrote a family creed that our oldest, Jane, has memorized and our one year old will begin reciting shortly. Here's an excerpt that Jane chants with a smile on her face,

> *"I was created to lead, serve, encourage and bring God's love, light, and joy everywhere I go.*
>
> *I am a winner and a champion.*
>
> *I will move a mountain with a shovel if that is what is required.*
>
> *When I get knocked down, I get back up. When I get knocked down again, I get back up again. I never quit.*
>
> *I never complain. I never make excuses.*
>
> *I take full responsibility for my life.*
>
> *I don't stand on the sidelines, I fight in the arena.*
>
> *I can and will change the world.*
>
> *I'm a Santmier!"*

This is how I am training my daughters. As a three year old, Jane is already developing a resolve to win coupled with a resolve to serve. More than that, she is determined to do whatever is required to make success come her way. When life knocks her down, she will get back up. When life knocks her down again, she will get back up again. She will never quit. She is resolved to be a champion. She is resolved, by the mere act of reciting these declarations every day, to win.

Do not settle for mediocrity. When you get knocked down, do not merely get back up only once so when life sucker punches you again, you say, "At least I tried and did my best." Never quit.

The word "resolve" means to decide firmly on a course of action. Let's not take these words lightly. To "decide firmly" means just that. Steel is firm. Steel doesn't bend or break easily. When we resolve within our inner being to win, we are deciding with a steel firmness, a firmness that doesn't bend or break, that we are going to win.

So who is winning? When you quarterback the sale, you are in it to win it for...your client! This game is not about your success or your fame—it's about your client successfully crossing into the endzone. We must have an insatiable desire for *our clients to WIN*! Nothing less will do. Quarterbacks don't step on the field to play catch or run around on the grass. They step on the field, laser-focused on getting that ball into the endzone as many times as possible.

What if Michael Vick, the best rushing quarterback in the history of the NFL, stepped on the field with the goal of improving *his own* quarterback rating? What if he had left the locker room every Sunday, focused on his success and the climb to the top of the quarterback rating chart? If you are not familiar with quarterback ratings, rushing yards and sacks are not included in determining the rating. If Vick wanted to improve his rating, all he needed to do was to stand in the pocket and only attempt a pass when he was sure he could connect with the receiver for at least 12.5 yards or more. (At this point, I'm losing some of you, but stay with me, because this applies to each of us!).

If Michael Vick played football so that *he* would win, in this case, to top the quarterback ratings, his team would lose and the ball would rarely reach the endzone. However, if Vick believed that winning directly correlates with getting the ball into the endzone, he would do what it takes to ensure it gets there. In Michael Vick's case, that would have meant running the ball—something that wouldn't have improved his quarterback rating at all.

As sales pros, we love winning, but many times, we do so at the expense of our clients. We run after personal success metrics that put us on the sales leader boards, but could potentially cause our clients to lose. When we focus only on ourselves, we are the only ones who reap the rewards of our work. If we continue on this path, we will eventually be the only ones on the field, and there will soon be no balls to quarterback down the field.

There is nothing wrong with wanting personal gain and success. I will be the first to admit that I want to attain success. I envision a million bucks entering my bank account every month...after tax deductions (yes, I envision a life where the IRS is irrelevant to me). But if I focus only on my personal success, I will soon be left on the field alone.

Here's the distinction we have to make: *In order for you to win, you must first focus on your clients winning.*

Michael Vick didn't care if he had a quarterback rating of zero. But if he consistently got the ball into the endzone, he knew he would have a job for the rest of his life (unless, of course, he did something stupid, like holding dog fighting brawls at his house).

The same is true for you and I. If we consistently focus on our clients winning, we will always have balls to quarterback, and our bankrolls will continue to grow.

Therefore, to quarterback the sale, you must have a resolve to help your clients win. You must envision them getting into the endzone, looking back down the field and saying, "That was it? Are you kidding? I thought this was going to suck, but this process was awesome! We did it! We bought a (home, car, investment product, fill in the blank)!"

Grit is the sludge in your gut that pushes you to keep going, and a resolve to win is the fire in your belly that gets you there! Again, when you decide to quarterback the sale, you are joining a group of professionals that collectively promise a consistent experience. Consistency is the key word. As my dad always told me, even a blind squirrel can find a nut once in a while. The trick is to produce the same result time and again for your clients. To do this, you have to keep that flame burning in your gut that is resolved to see your clients win! That flame can't die down or waiver, because if it does, your success too will waiver and die down with it.

Have you ever had a really good day when you got to the office and you were just ready to crush it? You took the first call, addressed the client's problem, and closed the sale in 5 minutes flat. The client was flabbergasted and immediately left you a Google review about their incredible experience. They posted a selfie on Instagram with one of those "shock and awe" faces, and within 24 hours, two of their friends had already reached out to you to purchase your product as well! (If you haven't had this experience, you soon will after you start quarterbacking your sales!).

Their friends call in, and once again, you hit the ball out of the park. You are on fire. Before you know it, you now have 6 more leads because of how great a job you've done getting the previous clients from snap to touchdown. You're ecstatic! The next morning you come in, and you're feeling the good vibes just like you did the previous day, but honestly, the flame is not burning quite as hot. You call 5 of the leads back from the previous day, but run out of time to call the 6th. You did a pretty good job, but let's be honest, you just closed more sales in the past 48 hours than you had in the past month! That one client you didn't call can wait until tomorrow…and complacency begins to set in.

Has this or a similar experience ever crept into your business? At large, every salesperson has been on this cycle. They are hungry because they have had a slow previous month, they ramp up activity which generates sales, referrals ensue, they post good numbers, following which they get complacent, have a bad month and then the cycle repeats itself.

This is a very selfish cycle that is based on the wrong kind of personal winning. When you are focused on personally winning and making money, you will live in this cycle of scarcity, hunger, success, complacency, and scarcity over and over again.

It is only when we have the resolve to help *our clients* win every single time that we continually produce consistent results. In other words, when we focus on personal money-making, we will produce inconsistent results for our clients. But when we focus on providing value to our clients and ensuring they win every single time, we will always have new mountains to climb and problems to solve.

Our desires change every day. One day, you may want to earn good wages, the next day, you may want to be a decamillionaire, and a month later, you may want to own a farm, produce all of your own food, and live off the grid. I know this cycle pretty well…This is the cycle of an entrepreneur, and too many entrepreneurial salespeople rely on their own needs and desires to run their business and sales cycles. Unless we want our business's graphs to look like rollercoasters, we shouldn't base our sales processes on personal resolve to win.

When we consistently solve other people's problems, we are not relying on personal motivation alone to do a good job. As we just established, our personal motivations keep changing. When we want our clients to win and we are solving their problems, we will deliver consistent results.

Motivation is Not Resolve

Resolve and motivation are two different beasts. Many sales professionals rely solely on being motivated in order to deliver their promised results. One day, he or she might wake up motivated to do a good job and deliver, and the next, sad and depressed with no desire to get out of bed, let alone go the extra mile for his/her clients.

If relied upon for success, our internal motivation will leave us unable to pay the bills one month and incredibly wealthy the next. Motivation is useful, but it is an unreliable and inconsistent source to drive quarterbacks. When we are ensuring our clients have a consistent experience of success, we cannot confuse resolve with motivation.

When a quarterback has resolve, it implies that he has an unwavering conviction that he will accomplish what he has set his mind to. Motivated or not, feeling it or not, he has a fire in his belly that is going to get that ball into the endzone. Taking action and ensuring our clients win puts money in our wallets and allows us to build our empires. Again, the quarterback's drive is consistent. Our internal motivation is not.

This brings us to the application. How do we develop a consistent resolve to help our clients win?

What is your client's win?

Before we look at developing a resolve, we must first define what a "win" is for our clients. In general, a win is simply solving their problem. In the analogy of the quarterback, this means getting them into the endzone! When a prospective client comes to you, they have a problem/s they would like you to solve. In order for them to win, all you need to do is solve their problem. This sounds simple enough, right?

The trick is finding the actual problem/s your clients are facing. I use the word *actual* intentionally. I sell insurance. One might think that my clients come to me to purchase an insurance policy. The majority of my competitors believe this, which leaves tremendous opportunities for me and my business to prosper. In your case, people might believe your clients are coming to you because they want to sell their old home, purchase a new home, get a loan with a low interest rate, or purchase investment products. This is simply the tip of the iceberg. What lies below the surface is the area where we're going to set ourselves apart and get the "win" for our clients.

In most businesses, there are several general problems that clients consistently have. Their problems generally lie one or two questions deeper than the surface. Therefore, in order to unearth our client's problems, we need to ask pointed questions. The questions we ask should be directed at determining the common problem our client is plagued with.

So what two or three problems do your clients typically face? What is the surface problem, and what are the most common problems below the surface that your client really cares about? The surface problem is simple. What product are you selling? Does your client want to buy a house, get a mortgage, or purchase an insurance policy? That's their surface problem. Their actual problem is their "why." Why do they want to buy a house? Why are they purchasing an insurance policy? Why are they getting a mortgage? When we ask the "why" question, we often discover our client's real problem. Sometimes, we may have to dig one or two more layers further, but when we find out why they are purchasing our products or using our service, we can determine the actual problem they want resolved. Here's how I practiced this exercise for my insurance business.

The surface problem most of my clients come to me with is that they need a homeowner's insurance policy. This is the tip of the iceberg. The context in which they are requesting an insurance policy helps me determine why they are shopping for insurance. For instance, if someone calls my office, currently owns a home in the area, and would also like a quote on her auto insurance, I know it is likely that she has one of two general problems: one, she believes her current insurance premium is to be high, or two, she has a problem with her current agent. Once I determine which camp she falls into, I ask one more question so she can clarify her specific problems. "Why do you believe your current rate is too high?" or "What problems are you facing with your current agent?" Ask and you shall receive. People love to talk about their problems. The real problem is that we often don't ask about their problems, and, therefore, we never hear them.

If, on the other hand, I receive a lead from a loan officer, I know that my client is purchasing a new home within the next 30 days or so. Their problems are very different. The two main problems these clients fall into are stress regarding the home purchasing process and distress about their new investment. If I know they are stressed, my goal is to take all of the worry off their plates. "How soon are you looking to close?" "Do you have any specific concerns about your new purchase?" By asking pointed questions, I can determine why they have come to me and how I can get them their win!

Develop a Resolve

How bad do you want it? How bad do you want your clients to win time and time again? How bad do you want the financial freedom that follows your clients' victories?

Winners' actions convey the degree to which they desire the victory. Peyton Manning used to practice even the simplest of moves such as taking a knee. He would repeat this motion of getting a snap and taking a knee over and over again until he couldn't get it wrong. Ben Roethlisberger wouldn't even allow himself to engage in other games that he knew he couldn't win. He wasn't going to leave room for losing.

What do your actions say about your resolve to win? Do you get up early? Do you practice your plays? Do you practice picking up and hanging up the phone? Do you look over every little detail of your process to ensure there aren't any cracks or inefficiencies?

When we have a resolve, we take action. We do not sit on the sidelines of life hoping everything goes according to plan. We act. So if you are currently in the land of inaction, admittedly not doing what you know you should, it is easy to determine that your resolve is lacking.

Clarity is what produces resolve. When we are crystal clear about what we want, we will do what is required to get the results we desire. We will be resolved to win!

I always have enjoyed weightlifting, but largely, my lifts have only marginally increased over the past decade. A year ago, I was really clear about what I wanted for my body. I listed out the things I wanted to accomplish and then wrote out the man (literally, the physical person) I would have to be in order to become the man I wanted to be. I realized that man was going to need to be strong but withstand the test of age. I knew I needed to build smart muscle mass and increase my flexibility so that I could powerfully stand on a stage in 30 years and deliver a one of a kind keynote on how I achieved my dreams and how my audience could achieve theirs.

This morning at the gym, I got under the squat rack and knew I had to push my legs beyond their limit. I wasn't motivated.

Instead, clarity brought me resolve under that iron. I wasn't lifting heavy and hard because I felt like it. I had no motivation to put myself in that much pain. I simply had a resolve to live my life a certain way, and that drove me to push my workout to the very max limit.

Clarity produces a clear resolve.

So what do you want out of life and business? If you could paint the perfect life, what would the portrait look like? I've already shared a portion of mine, but every day I have an image in my mind as I write out my goals. I imagine seeing a silhouette of me from the back, standing on a stage, spotlights on me, power walking and almost running, onto the stage. Electric, bass heavy music is pumping in the background, and people are clapping along with me to the beat. I am wearing a custom-made pinstripe suit with a high collared white shirt and silver cufflinks. From the back, you can see the width of my shoulders and the definition of my back as I clap. That's the man I want to become. That's what I envision.

To be quite honest, it doesn't matter *why* I want that, it just matters that I want that. For the longest time, I tried to find my "why" thinking that would produce a resolve in my gut to go out there and kill it. Over the past several years, I have stopped thinking about "why." I want this image to come to fruition and the image has slowly gotten clearer and clearer in my mind. I spend some time thinking about this event every day that in my mind, it has already happened.

Clarity has produced a resolve in my life and I believe it will produce a resolve in yours. What stands in the way are stories about what you believe or have been told you should do or who you should be. We all have them. Stories stifle us from our tapping into our true resolve. If we are not all in personally with what we are doing and what our path in life looks like, we will not have a resolve for our clients to win.

I was trained to be a pastor. I spent four years of my life studying the Bible so I could teach others about God, what He has done for them, and the hope He brings. But if I was honest with myself, I could never envision being a pastor. I didn't truly want to be a pastor. That occupation wasn't something euphoric in my mind--I just thought it was noble and a righteous career path. It wasn't until I was introduced to a godly man named Dan that my eyes were opened.

Dan saw an entrepreneur inside of me, took out a check book, and funded the birth of what I now know as my passion. He empowered me to start a business. Though that business never took off and actually failed, Dan's belief in me opened my eyes to who I was created to be. It took someone from the outside to look into my life and say, "Hey, you could be pretty good at business. Why don't you give that a try?" I needed a push. I needed a fresh set of eyes to help me clear back all the stories I had told myself about what a noble career path looked like. I needed a man to believe in me so much that he was willing to go out of his way to help me. It was Dan who opened my eyes to what I was created to do.

I believe in you, and I know there is something *you* were created to do. When we are honest with ourselves and we clear out all of the noise and stories we've been listening to, there's this beautiful core inside of us, a wiring if you will, that wants to produce something incredible. As for me, I had tried to paint a picture of how I thought I was wired (becoming a pastor), because I wanted my wiring to be spiritual and wanted to feel like I had purpose. But when I stripped back all of the stories and the picture I had been painting on my own, this image of me being a business owner and eventually speaking to thousands of people about my journey began to appear. I don't know *why* it began to appear: I just know that it did.

The more I continue to accept my passions and my wiring, all of the areas of my life start to come together. My marriage begins to thrive. I begin loving my two little girls like never before. My relationship with Jesus ironically grows, and my sales start to take off. When we stop denying who we were created to be, our lives begin to make sense and run like a well-oiled machine. And it is at this point, we can develop a true, deeply rooted resolve.

Clarity produced a laser-focused resolve in my life that has driven me to write this book, start a podcast, begin speaking in places I never thought possible, and push myself to higher limits in every single aspect of my life. And clarity will do the same for you.

Ask yourself this, what do you want? If you peel off the picture you've been drawing, what remains at the core? Who have you been created to be? Don't take it to heart if the answers don't come to you right away. Many of us have been denying ourselves what we wanted for so long and told ourselves so many stories to justify our existence that it may take months and years to peel back the layers to find your core. Life is a journey. And finding what truly gets you excited is worth pursuing.

Once you're clear, you will have a resolve to help your clients win, because as Zig Ziglar said,

"You can have anything in your life as long as you help enough people get what they want."

This quote is the essence of why we must become crystal clear about what we want prior to developing a resolve to help our clients win.

If you want to be successful, you must know what you want. We know that in order to get what we want, we must help others win, or get what they want. When we put it all together, we will have a consistent resolve to help our clients win. In short, get clear about what you want, find your client's "win," and then quarterback the sale over and over and over again.

Chapter 5
Confidence

It had been a grueling night. What was intended as the celebration of new life had become a night of hopeless and never-ending labor for my Lauren.

This was our first child, but we were prepared. We had gone to birthing classes where they re-taught Lauren and me how to breathe. It was weird at first to take in deep breaths with a dozen other confused soon-to-be mothers and fathers, but it felt right. We were in this together. We were learning how to successfully get through labor, and by the look on their faces, most of the guys had this in the bag! The instructor showed me how I could help Laur work through difficult contractions by holding her hips or rubbing her back. I felt prepared to help Lauren go through with her plan of a fully natural childbirth. I was confident that when the time came, I would be prepared.

It was a Friday afternoon, and Laur had her weekly doctor's appointment. The doc checked her and told her she was ready to deliver whenever she was ready. After hearing the great news, we felt it appropriate to celebrate at Taco Bell. And that was the straw that broke the camel's back. As they say, spicy does the trick, and right they were! That night, Laur went into labor.

Like a pro, Laur decided she would undergo labor at home before going to the hospital. Naturally, I felt the wisest choice was to go to sleep until she needed my help. After all, it was going to be a long night for me, and I didn't want to tucker out before the big reveal! Around two in the morning, Laur woke me up and informed me that she was indeed in labor and that we needed to start packing things to go to the hospital. I was on it! I jumped out of bed and started getting everything together. And then a subtle but very present thought came over me. Holy Crap! I was about to be a dad!

You might not remember it, but at 2:30 am on November 26th, 2014, the world stopped spinning.

As if freezing in the cold, I was shaking so bad I could barely pick the car seat up. I could feel the weight of reality descend into the backseat of our car as we raced to the hospital. I pulled it together and began doing mental repetitions, or reps, of all that the midwife and the birthing classes had taught me: take deep breaths, rub her back, and hold her hips (I swear this was exactly what they taught me: you can't make this stuff up!). In the back seat of the car, Laur was writhing in pain. But I calmly told her, "Just take deep breaths. When we get there I'll rub your back and hold your hips and everything will be okay." That was confidence.

We pulled up to the hospital, and Laur could barely walk. I picked her up out of the car and carried her into the hospital. What was happening? Everything was moving so fast, but time seemed to stand still! We got Lauren checked in and into a room. It was game time. Time to whip out my training.

And then she kicked me.

Laur, my beautiful sweet wife, literally kicked me and said, "Don't touch me!" It was like Mike Tyson said, *"Everyone has a plan until they get punched in the face."* What was I supposed to do now? I was equivalently punched in the face! I didn't learn this in my birthing classes! There wasn't an elective course on, "What to do when your wife kicks you and tells you can't do anything you learned" class. My confidence was now at level zero. I had no idea what to do to help my wife get through this excruciating pain.

There was a momentary silence before two doors flung open and my savior, as if bursting through the clouds, entered the room. Dr. Smith exuded confidence. His confidence was palpable. Before he arrived, I felt hopeless and my beautiful wife was going to have to push through this alone. But Dr. Smith knew what he was doing and took charge of the situation. He calmly spoke to Lauren and reassured her that today was going to be a beautiful day, a day she would remember for the rest of her life, but he just needed her to trust him. He reminded us that he had delivered over 5,000 babies and that this was not his rookie season. He was confident, but not in an off-putting way. His confidence brought peace to Laur. In a time of intense emotion, when we had no idea what to do, his confidence assured us everything was going to be okay. He knew what he was doing and helped guide us through the delivery of our first-born, Jane Elizabeth.

It was beautiful. Seeing Laur hold Jane for the first time is an image I will never forget. She wasn't in pain and was able to be present as Jane entered the world. Dr. Smith was very supportive of Laur's plan to have a natural childbirth and did everything in his power to help make that happen. But after 13 hours with no progression, Dr. Smith informed us that Lauren's contractions were actually not progressing labor at all. She was at a stalemate and hadn't made any progress for 13 hours. We thanked God for modern medicine and decided together that the next time we had a child (which would happen two years later), we were going to call in for an epidural on our way to the hospital.

Dr. Smith quarterbacked the delivery of my child. In a time of intense anxiety and every emotion under the sun, Dr. Smith's confidence allowed my daughter's delivery to be a beautiful memory we'll never forget.

I thought I had confidence. I thought that my preparation was adequate enough to support my wife through labor. But it wasn't. I had pseudo confidence.

Confidence can be found on a sliding scale between skills and self-belief. Quarterbacks have an inner confidence that is 50% skill-based and 50% self-belief-based. Many of us have the skill set but lack the personal self-belief to walk confidently. We tell ourselves stories about how our past successes can't determine future successes. We've been in our industry for five or ten years, yet still feel uncomfortable giving someone an exact answer. We are constantly hedging our bets in case a deal or process doesn't go perfectly. We hide under the guise of humility or modesty, but in reality, we lack self-belief that we are capable and professional.

Others lack the experience or skills, but have self-belief in droves. We can talk about how assured we are, and we genuinely mean it. But if we lack experience, we often find ourselves unable to meet the promises we have made to our clients.

On the sliding scale between ability and self-belief, confidence sits, waiting to be found, be put to use, and to produce instant results. So where does it lie?

Confidence is the feeling of self-assurance that arises from one's appreciation of one's abilities. When Dr. Smith stepped into that delivery room, I was assured, because I knew he knew what he was doing. Confidence is not only for one's own benefit: it also provides assurance to all those around.

During Super Bowl XLIII, the Steelers came out swinging. Big Ben led the team to a 20–7 lead and things were looking up. As quick as the tides could turn, the Arizona Cardinals took the lead. By the time there were two minutes and thirty seconds left on the clock, the scoreboard read 23–20. As Coach Arians recounts the story in his book, all eyes looked to Big Ben. "He was a picture of steely, cocksure, confidence…" Ben said, "We were built for this moment! We got this!'" And "got this" they did. Big Ben led a winning touchdown drive down the field, and the Steelers went home with the Vince Lombardi trophy in their hands.

Ben's confidence started within himself. He had to appreciate his own abilities and believe wholeheartedly that he was capable of winning. All of the practice, mental reps of this moment, and hard work brought Ben Roethlisberger confidence when he needed it most.

Our clients have a lot going on. There's no question that today's fast-paced society has brought more harm than good to our mental health. Anxiety, depression, and fear have become the status quo. Some studies have shown that over 18% of the American population has some form of diagnosed anxiety. To me, even this number seems low. The common cure is medication. "Take medicine," they say, "it will solve your problems."

What if you and I, simply by quarterbacking the sale, could decrease the stress levels in our clients' lives? Salespeople have the ability to provide real value and real solutions to people's problems. When we have resolve to help our clients win and the confidence to communicate it, we can take some stress off our client's plate. Quarterbacking the sale may alleviate some small stress in someone's life, but when we all begin to confidently address our client's problems, the effects will compound, and we can change the world together through sales.

Imagine a world where every purchase you had to make actually brought you peace. Imagine a banker who looked at your financial situation and said, "I got this." Imagine purchasing a home from a real estate agent who figured out exactly what you were looking for, gave you the luxury experience of a lifetime, and found the perfect house without you ever having to take time off work or search online one single time. Imagine a world where your lender gathered all your info in one sitting and met you at the signing table to close on time. Imagine a world where everyone loved insurance because it wasn't a hassle and the people they worked with were intuitive and did what was best for them at all times. Can you picture it?

Confidence is the key character trait that communicates that you have developed the grit and resolve to help your client win. Exude it, and you'll literally see your client's shoulders relax as they exhale a sigh of relief. Your clients want this relief. They live in a fast-paced world with even faster growing expectations. They are rooting for you to confidently solve their problems. They are rooting for you to be the hero who steps into their situation and improves their life. I'm rooting for you to be that hero. The world needs your confidence. The world needs all of us to quarterback the sale in our respective industries. When we do, we will see the compounding impact.

Developing Confidence

I found myself sitting around a table with 15 of the highest-paid executives and governmental leaders in Dayton. We were having breakfast on the top floor of the highest building in Dayton, Ohio. As I stared out of the windows at this exclusive view of the city, I thought to myself, *How in the world did I get here?*

I was 19 years old and had never stepped foot into any corporate business. I literally didn't even know what a boardroom looked like or how business people dressed for breakfast. I was brought up in a church. My dad was a pastor, and all I knew in the working world was inside those four walls of that Virginia church. I had never been on a sales call, been in a business meeting, or talked business with anyone outside of the church or a retail store.

And here I was, sitting next to the top business leaders of Ohio, wondering what to do.

I had started a small marketing company in Dayton that helped businesses give charitably while still getting a bang for their marketing dollars. I spent weeks calling over a 100 people a day out of my little apartment, hoping one person would say "maybe." After over a 1,000 calls through the yellow pages and Google searches, I was determined to get a yes. Michelle from PNC bank picked up the phone and agreed to throw me a bone.

I quickly found out that getting breakfast in the business world didn't really mean getting breakfast. As I ate my egg and cheese bagel, she sipped on her coffee, staring through my soul to find out if I was the real deal. I quickly put down my bagel sandwich and presented our service as if I had been doing it my whole life. The reality was that I had already made this pitch over a 1,000 times, so I was prepared. I just needed a little self-belief, and I had the winning formula for confidence.

Spoiler alert, I executed enough confidence in that breakfast meeting to score me that breakfast on the top of the skyscraper, one that even Michelle wasn't invited to. In a split second, the only self-assurance I needed to give myself was, "Look, you've already made this pitch a 1,000 times, you've got this."

It was through those early experiences that I developed confidence and learned out of necessity the importance of confidence in business and sales. I could recall hundreds of such stories, but the same lesson applies: confidence shows up when you've put the work in.

Self-belief is developed with physical reps. If you don't believe you can lift 100lbs, go out there and start lifting weights every day, over and over again, and you will soon believe you can lift 100lbs. Why? Because you physically lifted 100lbs.

Quarterbacks in the NFL aren't confident only because they've done mental exercises. They're confident because they've put the work in on the field as well.

In order to develop confidence, you've got to start putting in the reps. I already shared the story of Peyton Manning practicing taking a knee over and over again until he knew he couldn't mess it up. Why did he practice? Because he knew it would enhance his confidence when he stepped onto the field. He didn't want to lead his team down the field and have to worry about fumbling the ball when he took a knee in the last few seconds of the game.

We've already discussed the powerful role confidence can play in quarterbacking the sale. You can dramatically decrease the amount of stress and anxiety in your client's life by exuding, thereby assuring them of, confidence. But in order to develop this stress reducing, quarterbacking attribute, you've got to start putting in the reps.

Too many salespeople "fake it until they make it." What this really means is that they don't invest time into practicing their craft and decide to practice on their clients instead. Our clients deserve better. They deserve the confidence produced by experience.

Here are two of the biggest things my team and I do to get the reps in before quarterbacking the sale for our clients.

#1. Yellow Pages.

When a salesperson starts on my team, they do the exact same exercise I put myself through years ago. Start dialing for dollars. Don't fake it—just pick up the phone and try to get them to buy insurance. The success rate in this practice is very low. If they make even one sale off the yellow pages, I am thrilled. But after making a

1,000 calls, the confidence in their pitch and their offering grows, and they are ready to be set loose on the world.

#2. Role Play.

Every morning, my team and I role play sales calls for 15 to 20 minutes before we start calling prospects. We throw objections at one another and respond to potential scenarios we will encounter throughout the day. By the time we hop onto our first call for the day, we've already had several challenging "virtual" calls, so we are prepared for whatever may come on the other end of the line.

When you exude confidence when dealing with your client and tell them, "I got this," you take the stress and anxiety off their shoulders that often comes with purchasing your product or service. Confidence doesn't just come overnight. It is developed over time through reps. We each have the ability to speed up the development of our confidence by increasing the reps we do. As Peyton Manning and every great quarterback does, practice every aspect of your game off the field, so when you get on the field, you can confidently march your client into the end zone. Your client's anxieties and fears will be replaced by peace and joy, complements of your hard work and its resulting confidence.

Chapter 6

Humility

Winning quarterbacks put their team's success above their own. Coach Bruce Arians even goes as far as to say that if quarterbacks don't possess the invaluable trait of humility, they won't have a chance to make it in the league.

This is equally true in the field of sales and business. In his book *Good to Great*, Jim Collins studied top executives who took their good companies and made them great. Collins and his team were astonished to find that one of the top characteristics common in each great leader was a strong sense of humility: an inner desire to put their company and team before themselves. These top executives were more concerned about their company's success rather than their own personal riches or eminence. Collins recounts the stories of leaders who took pay cuts, differed personal pleasures and promotions, and consistently sacrificed their desires for the flourishing of their company.

But why? Doesn't this seem contradictory to the other key character traits such as confidence and resolve to win? In life, don't we need to put ourselves first, take care of ourselves over others, and guarantee our personal greatness and success first?

I am a fan of the Philadelphia Eagles. Growing up, I wanted to be just like my big cousin, Josh. Josh grew up in Philadelphia, while I was born in Virginia outside of Washington DC. When Josh and his family moved down to Virginia, I wanted to like whatever Josh liked! He was my big cousin after all! He had posters of the Philadelphia flyers in his room and was always talking about Philly this and Philly that! I didn't even know what Philly was. Was it a person, place, or a thing? But who cared? My big cousin Josh liked Philly, so I liked Philly!

One time when I was spending the night at Josh's house, I saw that he had a Philadelphia Eagles hoodie (or was it a shirt?), and I knew I had to up my game. I saved every penny I had, got a ride to Lids at the mall, and bought a $25 Philadelphia Eagles hat. That baby stepped my wardrobe game up to a 10! I was ready to go. Now the world could see that I was fan.

Donovan McNabb was the starting quarterback when I started watching their games on TV. He could fling the ball wherever he wanted and could stay in the pocket or scramble down the field. He was an excellent quarterback! From 2001–2005, McNabb led the team to five straight NFC Championship games, and in 2004, he led them to the Super Bowl. McNabb knew what he was doing.

Terrell Owens was McNabb's most talented receiver. Owens was a mammoth of a wide receiver and was able to make one of a kind catches. On the books, McNabb and Owens had one of the greatest quarterback/receiver relationships of all times, but pride tore them apart.

Each of the two wanted glory. Each wanted to get the credit for the team's successes, and neither player wanted to take credit for the failures of the team. They butted heads. The Philly tabloids would light up after every game, documenting (and commenting on) the daggers being thrown back and forth by them at each other.

When I look back at this relationship, it becomes clear to me that the reason for the demise of both their careers was self-centered pride. When a player focuses on his/herself-interests over those of the team, they are unable to do what is necessary to guarantee a win for the team. In fact, they often sabotage the team's victory if they do not get what they want. Owens would often throw temper tantrums if he felt the ball wasn't being passed to him enough. This caused disunity and brought the energy of the entire team down.

In both, football and sales, humility wins the game and ego-centric pride ruins it. The sales world is full of self-centered "go-getters" who will fumble anyone in their way of getting what they want. Many salespeople are demeaning in the way they speak to others. When they walk into a room, they believe others should come talk to them and they should be sought after for a conversation. Though this sort of behavior initially feels good to the proud man or woman, it causes others to feel inferior and have zero desire to engage in conversation or business. As the old saying goes, be careful how you treat people on the way up, because you might meet them again on your way down. Pride comes before the fall.

Pride not only falsely inflates one's self worth, but it also diminishes the worth of others. Donald Miller, in his book *Building a Story Brand*, notes that our clients want to be the heroes in their own stories. As sales professionals, our tendency is to want to be the hero, not just in our own story, but in our client's story as well. We want them to remember us, think we're awesome, and like us so much they tell all of their friends about us! We tell them all the reasons they should do business with us. We have handouts, email campaigns, and thousands of social media posts that point out how awesome we are and why no one else is as good as we are at what we do.

Miller points out that our clients are looking for a guide. They are looking for an expert to come into their story and help them become the hero. Our clients want us to help guide them to a climactic peak where they can stand and shout, "I've done this!" But how often do we as sales professionals lead our clients to that "climactic peak," the end zone, closure of the sale, and yell, "Look at what I've done! Aren't I the most incredible salesperson the world has ever seen?"

Just like Terrell Owens and Donovan McNabb, when we seek glory for ourselves above the needs of our clients and organizations, we will be incapable of reaching our highest level of success. It seems paradoxical, but when we focus on others, we win. Being the quarterback for our clients requires humility.

"You can get anything in life you want if you will just help enough other people get what they want." Zig Ziglar

Kimberly-Clark, the paper company that owns brands such as Huggies, Kleenex, and Scott Toilet Paper, was a pretty good company. Everything was running smoothly. The company performed at an average level among competitors and owned many printing mills, which made for a profitable business. But they weren't great.

Darwin Smith was an aspiring young lawyer looking to get some corporate experience. He began his career at Kimberly-Clark in 1958 and eventually worked his way up the ladder to become the Chief Executive Officer, a title he held for 20 years. When Smith took the helm in 1971, stock prices of the company were $2.10 a share. By the time he retired in 1991, stock prices had escalated to well over $21 per share. What's even more impressive is that stock prices continued to increase after he left Kimberly Clark as well. Smith not only lead a company from Good to Great, points out Jim Collins in his book, but laid the foundation for further growth of the company after he was gone.

Look up the name Darwin Smith, and you'll be hard-pressed to find many articles or references to this great CEO. But by the time of his retirement, Kimberly Clark was beating Proctor and Gamble in 6 out of 8 categories! Smith could care less if anyone knew his name. He could quite frankly care less if anyone knew Kimberly Clark's name. However, Darwin Smith cared deeply about whether the company was successful and if the world used its products. His ambition was first and foremost focused on the success of his company.

Collins recounts stories of what Smith's co-workers had to say about him. Phrases like, "He was rather self-effacing," "Didn't believe his own clippings," or "He was a simple man," were repeated time and time again. Darwin Smith even said of himself, "I never stopped trying to become qualified for the job."

Stop and think about this phrase for a moment: Darwin Smith, CEO of a major company for 20 years, "never stopped trying to become qualified for the job!" Steve Jobs echoed this never-ending pursuit of improvement in his speech to Stanford graduates: "Stay hungry and stay foolish." This humility, on display, is what led to the exponential growth of their companies and set them on the path of further progress even after both of these men were gone.

We live in an ego-driven society that screams, "Whoever has the biggest ego wins!" But history proves this is a lie. The person with the biggest ego can certainly make a lot of money. He/she can have a big house and achieve some success, but pull out the ego-driven, self-centered leader, and everything they've worked hard to build evaporates into thin air. Why? Because the growth was all centered around them!

Pride leads to a life and a business that crumbles. When we use others to selfishly promote ourselves and our desires and we abuse our power, we will eventually fall to our ruin. Our team members and clients will have no desire to speak to us, because they know that as soon as we open our mouth, we're just going to talk about ourselves. The lie we can find ourselves hearing is that pride attracts others. We begin to believe that pride will make others think we're self-confident, that we have your heads on straight, and that we know what we're doing. This couldn't be further from the truth. *Pride is a stench that repels, never attracts.*

In sales, we have the privilege of providing value to the world. When you started your career, you had to either deeply believe in the solution you were selling or fake it till you made it. However, at this point in your career, I hope you have found a product or service that you genuinely believe solves a real need in the marketplace. I hope you have found that true wiring we discussed previously. During every sales call you make, you have the power to bring value to your customer. You have the ability to look across the table and say with absolute confidence, "I can make your life better today."

If we allow pride to sneak in, our client will hear, "I can make your life better today…so that I can benefit." There are many salespeople that get away with this sort of narcissistic behavior, but their process leaves their clients feeling used as means to an end. In any business where referrals are paramount, pride will work us out of jobs. We may close a deal, but we will simultaneously close our pipeline.

I was recently at a real estate happy hour and was introduced to a real estate agent who claimed to be quite a hustler. He lived up to the hype. For a consistent thirty minutes, this guy couldn't stop talking about himself. It also didn't help that I was baiting him.

The best way to tell if someone is a narcissist is to ask them how business is going and see how long it takes before they return the question back to you. This guy fell for it hook line and sinker. He got so excited about his business that he started pitching to me before even knowing what I did for a living.

He said, "Let me show you how well business is going. I'll pitch to you right now and see if I can make you want to list your house with me!" "Shoot!" I responded.

"Hi, my name's Grant and I sold $11 million worth of homes in my first year of business. I know how to help you get the maximum amount of money out of this house. Tell me how much would you like for it, and I'll show you how I can ring it out of your house?"

I wasn't going to hold back with this guy. I wanted to see how arrogant he really was. "If you don't mind me saying, I don't think I'd buy or list my house with you. You kind of come across a bit cocky." Without skipping a beat, he continued for another five minutes about why I should list my house with him "today!"

We are working toward leading our clients into the end zone, but if it's all about us, we'll never be able to help them achieve their "win." How many times have you heard a salesperson say, "They just won't get the paperwork in to me," or, "They won't return my calls"? Could it be that the problem lies within us? What if we are in this for ourselves and our clients sense it? What if they don't feel like the hero in their story, but like a supporting character that doesn't have significance? If they were made to feel like royalty, and they had the assurance that we were going to solve their problems, would that incentivize them to get moving a bit quicker?

We need to come to grips with one of the truest facts of life: *our clients only care about themselves and their problems.* That's it. They don't care about what we think, how good we are, or how many deals we closed last year. They don't care about how big our house is, the sort of car we drive, or why we believe we are the best. They care about where *they* are going and how we can help them get there.

Salespeople can play themselves up so much in the sales process that their prospects clam up and eventually fade out of their pipeline. Arrogant people seem unapproachable. It's completely useless to have a conversation with them and to try to interject with your thoughts, opinions, or problems. When we appear egoistic in the sales process, our clients don't talk—they simply smile and nod. The fact is, they may be genuinely impressed by us because what we rattled off about may actually be quite impressive. But, they won't actively engage in a dialogue with us. They don't care about what we've done, even though they may appreciate it. They may even tell us how impressed they are, but on the inside, they do not care about what we have to say about ourselves or how credentialed we are. They are concerned with their problems only. They want to be the hero in their own story and be guided to their desired nirvana by you.

A quarterback constantly asks him/herself, "How can I celebrate, honor, and elevate my client so they feel like the hero in this storyline? How can I ensure they get into the endzone while being genuinely excited about what they accomplished throughout the journey?"

The test of a humble quarterback is after the client has entered the endzone. When people are cheering, are they chanting your name or your client's? Is the spotlight solely focused on you, or are you standing at the side, celebrating your client's accomplishment with the rest of their friends and family?

Humility isn't sexy and it isn't natural in the sales world, but true quarterbacks humbly guide their clients and make their clients the hero of their storyline. Pride creates a barrier between you and your client that you might not even be aware of. When you display arrogance, your client ceases to communicate with you. Humbly putting the client's needs ahead of your own guarantees your client wins, and ensures that your business lasts the test of time. Humility is the foundation upon which lasting legacies of success are built.

Chapter 7

Empathy

Have you ever met a real life quarterback? Almost 99% of the time, quarterbacks have typical Type A personalities. People with Type A personalities are typically ambitious, proactive, outgoing, impatient, competitive, and result-oriented. Empathy does not typically feature in their top 5 strengths in their StrengthFinder exam results. In general, a common flaw among quarterbacks and salespeople is they lack the ability to slow down and see what is happening around them. This can cause them to be blindsided when a deal goes bad or a play falls apart, when in reality, if they would have picked up on some subtle cues earlier on, they would have realized that their client or teammate was never fully on board or present throughout the deal or play.

Empathy (Webster Definition): *"The action of understanding, being aware of, being sensitive to, and vicariously experiencing the feelings, thoughts, and experience of another of either the past or present without having the feelings, thoughts, and experience fully communicated in an objectively explicit manner."*

Did you get all of that? Me neither. Let's break it down so we can understand this definition fully and how it applies to us successfully quarterbacking the sale.

Before we dive into this topic, I need to make a blanket statement: though this does not apply to everyone, women are generally more empathetic than men. Their sensitive and nurturing spirit allows them to feel what others around them are feeling. Therefore, men, we have a greater need to wrap our brains around this attribute. The women who read the definition above probably just nodded their heads and said, "Yes! Preach! That's right!" whereas the men reading the definition probably scratched their heads and said, "Maybe I'll just skip this chapter…" So men, let's learn from the ladies here, and ladies, go on and teach the men around you how to be a little more empathetic. Let's break down this detailed definition together

First, empathy is an action. When one is truly empathetic, they say or do something such that the person or people they're empathizing with experience their empathy. We can't merely try and feel what someone else is feeling. We must take that feeling and tastefully communicate it back to our clients.

Second, empathy implies understanding, being aware of, being sensitive to, and vicariously experiencing something being experienced by another. Someone who is an empathetic leader is focused on others. They work to fully understand the situation and experience their client is going through as if they were walking in their client's shoes. Empathetic salespeople are also sensitive to their client's life, careful not to push them in a direction that exacerbates their woes.

"…feelings, thoughts, and experience of another of either the past or present…" When big macho men think about empathy, they often get stuck up on "feelings." Empathy involves more than just one's feelings. Maybe your client has a thought that you need to be aware of. If you can tell by their facial expressions that something isn't quite right, that's empathy. Maybe your client just got into a car accident. As an insurance agent trying to smooth out the situation, you are not just getting involved with their feelings, you're actually working to understand what happened to them and why they are flustered by their current circumstances.

The key distinction we as sales pros need to implement into our empathetic skills is the "past or present" component. Maybe your client had a really bad experience with a real estate agent in the past. We should empathize with their past negative experiences, even if we are distanced from it. Empathy thrusts us into our client's life, not to just soak in the surroundings of the present, but to understand, be aware of, and be sensitive to the context of our client's life that has led them to this present moment. Empathy makes you the best detective. It enables us to take into consideration every little nook and cranny of our client's life so that we can show them we are fully present and engaged in their journey, while looking out for them every step of the way.

In a vein similar to humility, empathy demonstrates that we are looking out for and concerned about our client's wellbeing and not just pursuing our own personal agenda.

"...without having the feelings, thoughts, and experience fully communicated in an objectively explicit manner." Men, this is where it gets tricky for us. We are black and white creatures. When someone says something, we take what they said at face value. Even when they don't say anything, we take their silence at face value. We don't read further into the situation.

However, it is important that we do, and this is where men can learn from their female counterparts. Being empathetic is not about asking a dozen questions. It's about instinctively picking up on non-verbal cues our clients give us. They may have had a bad experience with a previous agent in the past, but we can only understand how that made them feel based on their non-verbal cues, not through objectively explicit communication.

Empathy is about feeling what others feel, and that's why assessing how empathetic we are is such a tricky task. "Feeling," to begin with, is subjective. If I stub my toe, I may verbalize my pain and yell, but on the inside, I am *feeling* disappointed that I broke my grandma's lamp. The outsider seeking to empathize with my pain, such as my wife, may ask, "Are you alright? I've stubbed my toe on this very lamp and man did it hurt! I feel your pain!" The sentiment is sweet, and she was trying to be empathetic. She was relating what she thought I was feeling to a similar experience she had had in the past. According to her, she was being empathetic. But to me, she wasn't successfully empathizing with how I was actually feeling. She was simply projecting what she thought I was feeling and empathizing based on her subjective experience.

This same scenario happens with our clients. I have had the privilege of providing homeowner's insurance to a lot of first-time homebuyers. During the home buying process, there are so many emotions spinning around. When we began working with first-time homebuyers, we worked our butts off to make the process incredibly fast. We've made it so fast and efficient that our buyers can simply talk to us for five minutes or less, e-sign an application, and walk into closing the deal. I thought every homebuyer would want to get their insurance process out of the way as quickly as possible. Over the years I have realized that though most of our clients simply want speed, others get even more stressed out when things are moving too quickly.

Many of my clients have been saving up for years in order to buy their first home. They have envisioned what this process would be like and they, oddly enough, are excited to deal with the process of the homeowner's insurance. They don't want to rush the process. They certainly want the process to be efficient, but they also want to go over every little minutia of the policy.

If I, with my Type A personality, plow through my extremely efficient process without listening to and empathizing with the client, we may get ready to sign the application and they may respond with, "I'm not interested anymore." As salespeople, our typical response is, "Is there anything I could have done differently? If you don't mind me asking, why did you decide to go somewhere else?" People typically reply, "No, nothing was wrong, I just decided to go with "X" company because (fill in the excuse)." They can't place a finger on what you specifically did wrong, because at the end of the day, you just took them through the highly efficient process that you've taken hundreds or thousands of clients through. The process was great and efficient, but the experience and the feeling it gave them missed the mark.

Empathy is the X factor in effectively quarterbacking the sale.

When a quarterback is in the huddle with his team, he and his play caller have a plan. They know what play they want to run and have valid reasoning backing their choice. When a quarterback just runs with the play without any regard for what went on in the huddle, the play has the potential to collapse. When good quarterbacks call the play, they are acutely aware of what their teammates are feeling. Do they know the play? What does the look on their face say? Are they down in the dumps, feeling like they can't win or score a touchdown? It's the quarterback's job to assess the huddle, and be empathetic and work to understand where his teammates are coming from. It's the quarterback's role to be empathetic to his teammates as they march down the field.

I was interviewing the head coach at our local high school who played in the quarterback position at the collegiate level for five years. He recounted a lesson he learned from one of his coaches, "If I noticed my players were taking the game a little too seriously or they were down and discouraged, I would say, 'Look at that cheerleader in the endzone. Let's get a closer look, huh boys?' And then the guys would chuckle and would be able to relax and just execute the play."

That's empathy: being acutely aware of what is happening in the lives of the people around us, meeting them where they're at, and guiding them to their desired destination.

Developing Empathy

Wouldn't it be nice if everyone just said exactly what was on their mind, specifically how that made them feel, and how we could precisely help solve their problem? Yes, it would be convenient, but it would take all the fun out of the game of selling!

My wife and I love playing the "backstory" game. We go out to eat, and when we see an interesting looking couple, we take turns making up stories about them. "He grew up on a farm and decided yesterday he was going to make a Tinder profile and go out with the first person who swiped right," I'll start his backstory and Lauren delves right into hers. "She's always wanted to be a model, but is color blind. She decided she would take up knitting instead, and when she heard that her boyfriend from high school was single, she put her pigtails in and tracked him down. She wants six kids and he wants one, but he is playing along with the big family thing so she stays interested in him." Who knows, maybe you've been one of our infamous backstory contestants.

This is obviously a dramatic way to segue into being empathetic, but have fun with it. Get to know your clients, and try and make a game of how many non-verbal cues you can pick up on. I think one of the biggest barriers to being empathetic is that we take it so seriously. Being empathetic doesn't mean only feeling the bad and the depressing parts of our client's life. We can also relate to our client's joys and exciting backstories that have led them to us!

Empathy is a powerful way to connect with your client so that you can continue to anticipate their every need before they verbally communicate it. Picking up on the little nuances shows them that you care and allows for a genuine connection. It allows you, as the quarterback, to call audibles, change the play up, or call a timeout if you need to make a course correction in your sales process.

As we approach the end of Part 1, Mindset of a Quarterback, I'd highly recommend taking a StrengthsFinder 2.0 exam on Gallup's website. In this exam, you will discover your top five strengths. You'll also see the traits that are not your strengths. And my guess is that if you're reading this book and you identify as a Type A personality, empathy is not going to be near the top of your list.

Part 2

Playbook of a Quarterback

Chapter 8

Initiative

Quarterbacks don't wait for the ball to tell them where it would like to go. Quarterbacks take the initiative and get the ball down field as quickly and as seamlessly as possible. Your goal is for your client to get into the endzone, look back down the field and ask, "Was that it? That was way too easy!" When you experience this moment with a client, celebrate. You have just quarterbacked the sale!

At the core of this entire quarterbacking philosophy is *initiative*. Initiative is the opportunity to act or take charge before others do. Initiative is proactive, not reactive. When we find ourselves reacting to problems as they fly past us, it is easy to get frustrated and feel like the client is "high maintenance" or is being needy. However, being reactive is a red flag indicating that you are not taking the initiative and your process needs to be changed.

Many of you reading this book are connected in some way to the real estate industry. We often get too comfortable with the way things are that we don't realize we are dropping the ball or we've stopped going the extra mile for our clients. As an exercise, let's take a look at the real estate transaction to see the role initiative plays in the sales process.

The Jones' Un-Quarterbacked Experience

Jim is an excellent real estate agent. He's been selling real estate for about two years and has started to see some success. He loves his work and does everything in his ability to make the transaction as hassle-free and enjoyable for his clients. (Isn't that what we all want life to be? Hassle-free and enjoyable?) Last week, Jim was showing the Jones a house on Elm street and he sent them a link to the property address to meet him there at 2:00 pm. On the way, the Jones got a flat tire and had to call AAA to get a spare put on. This obviously caused the Jones to be late for the appointment, and by the time they reached the house at 3:15 pm, Jim wasn't the only real estate agent there.

There was a second showing with another perspective buyer at 3:30 pm, and the second real estate agent had shown up early to prepare the house for his showing. Jim pleaded with the other real estate agent to let him and the Jones quickly walk through the house and then promised to leave and be on their way. Jim assured him that they wouldn't stay longer than 10 minutes, and he kindly agreed to Jim's plea.

The Jones *really* liked the house. In fact, when they walked through the front door, Mary Jones said those marvelous words, "I could see myself living here!" Jim was ecstatic! The four-month courting process was about to culminate in a sale! Or so it seemed, but Jim had to quickly finish the tour of the house as the second real estate agent coughed loudly at the front door.

It was time to leave, but Jim was confident that with words like, "I could see myself living here," he was going to close this deal and get this couple moved into their new house! "Let's meet in my office," Jim said. "We'll talk through the house and discuss if you'd like to make an offer on this home!" With a big grin on their faces, the Jones agreed and hopped into their car and followed Jim back to his office.

They walked into Jim's office and were greeted by a desk covered in papers—papers that looked pretty important. The Jones helped Jim move the papers off the desk that had migrated to the chairs they were supposed to sit on, and quickly sat down to write up an offer.

They submitted their offer, but it was too late. The couple who had seen the house right after them had submitted an offer, apparently faster than the Jones were able to, and the other real estate agent had somehow gotten the property locked down. Jim was crushed as were the Jones. And the deal fell through.

Several weeks later, things went their way, and they got a decent house under contract. Not their dream home, but it wasn't a bad second option. After the home was under contract, Jim, feeling he was taking the initiative, called the Jones to inform them they needed to get a loan finalized, an inspection scheduled, and homeowner's insurance for their new house. Hanging up the phone, Jim said to himself, "Boy am I on top of this! The Jones don't know how lucky they are to get such a proactive real estate agent!"

Two weeks passed, and Jim thought he should check in to see how everything was going. The Jones picked up the phone, and it almost sounded like they were upset. Jim asked them what was wrong, and the Jones responded, "Nothing." Jim reassured them that if they needed anything, anything at all, they could let him know, and he would be on it! Once again, proactive Jim felt pretty good about himself. He was on top of the deal!

Four weeks passed, and Jim was starting to get worried. He hadn't heard from the mortgage company on a closing date, and the Jones hadn't reached out to him since they last spoke. What was going on? Jim called the Jones once again, and this time, the tone was unmistakable. "How are things?" Jim asked. "How are things? HOW ARE THINGS?" Mary blurted out. "Things are not good, Jim. Not good. Our mortgage guy said he didn't have the right paperwork, and so we're held up there. The house ended up being in a flood zone, or so the lender tells us, so we need to get flood insurance. The inspection came back with a lot of issues that we're really not sure what to do with." "Wait a second, you already had your inspection? You didn't tell me that. Did you have an appraisal as well? Which mortgage company are you working with? What's their phone number? I'll get this straightened out. Don't you worry. I'll get it all sorted out for you," Jim panicked and blurted out.

Several weeks later, after many long sleepless nights, the Jones' closed on their home. After they finished signing the paperwork, the Jones' shook Jim's hand, said a simple "Thank You," and were on their way, never to see Jim again.

Don't Drop The Ball

Obviously, this is a dramatic example, but as painful as this is to say, I think we've all seen a very similar story unfold at some point or the other. When we don't take the initiative in the sales process, we end up being inactive. We end up having to backpedal and retrace our steps. If we want to make a difference, and truly level up our sales game, we have to take the initiative and act before our clients do.

In other words, don't drop the ball! Every time we ask our client to take the initiative in the sales process, we are essentially putting the ball down on the ground and asking the ball to decide on its own where it would like to go and what play it would like to call. When put this way, it sounds ridiculous, but the sad reality is that a majority of sales professionals do this with their clients every day. They think they are doing their client a favor by giving them "space," but in reality, they are dropping the ball and opening up the sales process to a litany of problems.

Every time the ball is dropped, there is an opportunity for it to roll wherever it wants. Have you ever rolled a football? If you haven't, go get a football, and try to roll it across the room to a specific target. When you roll a football, it goes all over the place, and you cannot predict where it will end up!

The same is true of our clients. When we drop the ball and ask them to take the initiative, there is no telling where they are going to end up or what unforeseen problems they might encounter. If you're like Jim, it won't end well for you or them.

Quarterbacks lead the play. They take the initiative and are proactive. Some may counter this and say that this is too controlling. "Our clients should be able to make the decision they feel is best for them. I don't want to come across as controlling or pushy!" It is true. If you were to merely dominate your way through the sales process, you would certainly be put on the blacklist, and your services would never be used again. However, if you have the mindset of the quarterback and you lead with confidence, humility, and empathy, your client will be the happiest camper alive.

When our intentions are pure and we genuinely want to lead our clients through a positive sales experience, we can confidently quarterback every aspect of the sale. You have something valuable to offer to the world and therefore, can confidently direct your clients down the field using the string of plays you've determined that give them the best chance of getting into the endzone as quickly and painlessly as possible.

Our clients won't fault us for taking the initiative if it is in their best interest. We do what we do every single day. I don't want to go to the surgeon, tell them I need shoulder surgery, and then instruct them on which knives to use and where to make the cut.

That wouldn't end well. As sales professionals, we are experts who are expected to know what we are doing. Therefore, we can confidently quarterback and lead every aspect of the sale, right down to driving the client to their new house.

The Jones' Quarterback Experience

What if Jim had quarterbacked the sale? Let's write a new story for the Jones.

Jim is an excellent real estate agent. He has been selling real estate for about two years and is starting to see some success. Last week, Jim was showing the Jones a house on Elm Street. He scheduled the showing for 2pm and informed the Jones that he would pick them up from their house at 1:30 pm to personally take them to the showing. When the Jones got into the car, Jim had hot cups of their favorite Starbucks coffee sitting in the cup holders. How did he know their favorite type of coffee? Because he had taken the initiative to ask them some "getting to know you questions" at their first meeting.

"Wow! Thanks for the coffee, Jim! That's funny, we were just about to ask if we could swing by Starbucks before heading to the house!" Sam Jones exclaimed. "Well, I'm glad I could beat you to it! Who's ready to go see their dream home?" Jim said.

Jim pulled up to the house, and before they got out of the car, he informed them that there was a 3:30 pm showing scheduled after them, so they would have about an hour and a half to look through the house if they'd like. "This one is going to go fast," Jim told them "It just went on the market last night, and there have been showings all day. In case you like it, I've brought the paperwork with me to get an offer submitted as soon as possible. Let's have a look!"

The Jones really liked the house. In fact, when they walked through the front door, Mary Jones said those marvelous words, "I could see myself living here!" Jim was ecstatic! This four-month process was about to culminate in a sale!

"What do you think? Would you like to make an offer on this house?" Jim asked.

"Are you kidding me? This is the perfect house! This is what we've been looking for the past four months! Yes! We'd love to not only make an offer, but guarantee this house is ours!" Mary said, almost yelling.

"Perfect! Congratulations! Here's the paperwork, give me a quick second, and we'll get everything written up and submitted to the listing real estate agent!" Jim was on it. And just like that, the home was theirs! The offer Jim submitted was so strong that the listing real estate agent quickly responded with an affirmative yes, and the home was under contract!

That evening, Jim called the Jones to tell them the exciting news. The Jones were ecstatic! "Thank you so much! We're so happy to be moving into our new home!" "I'm excited to get you moved in as well. Tomorrow morning, I've set up breakfast at Stacy's Diner, because I know you all love that place. I work with a fantastic Loan Officer who delivers every single time for my clients and makes financing your new home a breeze. He will be at our breakfast and will help get the ball rolling to finance this house! I'll email you a list of things he will need you to bring tomorrow morning, and then I'll meet you there at 8 am. Does that work?"

"That would be perfect!" the Jones said together. The next morning, breakfast went smoothly, and toward the end of breakfast, two other professionals walked up and congratulated the Jones on their new home. Jim stood up and introduced them. "Mr. and Mrs. Jones, this is Terra and John. Terra is my most trusted insurance agent, who continually delivers exceptional service for my clients. She will help put together a customized homeowner's insurance policy for your new home, and it will only take about 15 minutes. John is a home inspector whose reputation for leaving no stone unturned has made him one of the best inspectors in the state. After we finish our breakfast, I'd like to schedule a time for him to inspect the house with you. Does that sound good to you all?"

Sam and Mary could barely believe it. Wasn't the process of purchasing a house supposed to be stressful and dragged out endlessly? So far, the most stressful part of their homebuying process was trying to determine if they wanted sausage or bacon with their eggs. Within a couple weeks, the Jones closed on their house and couldn't stop telling all of their friends about the excellent experience Jim had given them. And of course, how much they loved their new home!

Do you see it? Do you see how taking the initiative alters your client's experience? I would want to buy a house with Jim a second time just to experience that concierge service. Who cares about the house! I want to feel like a king! The sales process becomes pure indulgence: a marriage of bliss and excitement! When we take the initiative, we never have to be reactive. We never have to backpedal to dig ourselves out of the mess we've created. Our clients will become loyal to us beyond reason.

With my team, I take the initiative one step further. I call it providing a concierge level of service, and it's one of the pillars of our brand promise. Have you ever been in a five-star restaurant or a top-tier hotel? Yes, these people take the initiative, but they do more than take work off your plate. They know your next move before you make it and deliver a solution that makes you feel like royalty.

In every part of our sales process, as we quarterback the sale, our goal should be to make our clients feel like royalty. They are valuable to us, and we want to go above and beyond to make their lives that much better. Jim provided this level of service when he anticipated that the Jones would want coffee and had it ready for them piping hot when they got into the car. In my line of business, we don't ask our clients to do any work after the sale. We get all of the paperwork to the right people while they just sit back and relax. We could wait for them to call to let us know that their insurance rates went up dramatically, but would I want to get that call from the Queen of England? Absolutely not! I would be embarrassed! So we take the initiative, treat them like royalty, look over their policies on their behalf—every single renewal—and then resolve any problems before they even get a notification from the insurance company.

When our processes are laced with initiative, we will prevent ourselves being less reactive and blindsided by unforeseen problems. Our clients will feel like royalty, and the transaction will go smoothly every single time. Our clients want this concierge level of service. They want us to take the initiative. Initiative is the foundation for building a winning sales process, which is what we'll dive into next.

Chapter 9

Level Up Your Playbook

Bruce Arians, the then offensive coordinator for the Steelers, had a dynamite young quarterback on his hands. Ben Roethlisberger was a mammoth of a man who wasn't afraid to stand in the pocket a little longer and risk getting pummeled by a 350-pound defensive end. His athleticism was a thing to behold. He was special, and Arians knew it.

Up until that point in Roethlisberger's young career, most of the plays had been called by his coaching staff. But things were about to change.

Arians took Roethlisberger out golfing and sat down with his team's leader. Over a cocktail, Coach Arians told Ben, "I'd like you to help me rewrite the playbook. If you show me you can handle it, I'll let you call the plays." And handle it he did.

Roethlisberger took complete ownership of the playbook and meticulously combed through every single play. He got rid of some plays, added some new ones, and renamed old plays so he could communicate them more effectively. Roethlisberger leveled up his playbook.

The second sphere of quarterbacking is your processes; in other words, your playbook. Effective quarterbacks don't wing plays.

They don't get onto the field and say to one receiver, "Run straight down the field," and to another, "Run out to the right and let's see what happens!" They have an intentional set of plays and know exactly which ones to string together to score a touchdown.

You currently have a playbook, whether you are aware of it or not. Every salesperson and business leader has a typical way of doing business. For example, when someone calls you, you instinctively say, "Hello, this is Zach, how can I help you?" Or when you present a proposal, you like to go to your prospect's office with a three-ring binder and present your thoughtfully articulated proposal.

Line up Ben Roethlisberger, Peyton Manning, and Tom Brady, and you'll see three physically different quarterbacks. They have different body types, strengths and weaknesses, and likes and dislikes. If Ben Roethlisberger were to copy Tom Brady's playbook, I'd argue that he would be far less successful when playing by his own playbook. Why? Because he is an entirely different quarterback with different strengths and weaknesses.

The same is true for you and designing your own playbook. There is only one of you. Yes, different quarterbacks may have stylistically similar playbooks, but there will always be one-off plays that are crucial for you to score a touchdown that you can do better than anyone else in the entire world. All it takes is discovering what those plays are and putting the time and effort into designing your unique playbook. So that's what we're going to do.

Outline Current Playbook

We are creatures of habit, and over time, our habits become our playbook or the process we use to do business.

What separates a successful salesperson from the average salesperson is the effectiveness and intentionality of their playbook.

Is every play necessary? Does every play fit into the overall strategy of getting the ball into the endzone? Are there plays where my client may need to take the initiative and run down the field on their own? Are there plays I don't use that I should implement? If so, what part of my playbook needs to be adjusted and how should I adjust it? These questions will get us started as we outline your current playbook.

Before we begin, it is extremely important that you leave all your emotions or opinions at the door. You are not trying to justify your process or insert a commentary to explain the certain way you do things. You are simply going to be writing down your playbook from start to finish in excruciating detail.

When I say excruciating detail, I really mean it. In order for you to get as much out of this exercise as possible, you cannot leave any stone unturned. It may be tempting to create categories and check steps off your list. For instance, your first step may be: "Client walks into the store and associate greets him or her."

Good start, but we're about to get a lot deeper. The devil is in the details, and quarterbacks are relentless in their pursuit of excellence. This means that we make sure every little part of our process is accounted for and intentional. Instead of the above statement, consider outlining your first step like this:

"Client walks into the showroom through two black doors that are propped open by wooden wedges. Subtle perfume is pumped toward the opening of the door, and lights are at 75% capacity. Client first sees a display table with multi colored shirts and sweatshirts with jeans on the right side. The cloths are placed on an off-white table and looks about 15 years old. An associate is standing on the right side of the door dressed in clothing that can be purchased from the store and is wearing a name badge on his left breast with his first name engraved on it. The associate makes eye contact with the customer, extends his right hand for a handshake, and says, 'Good afternoon, I'm Sam, have you been here before?'"

Do you see the difference? Why in the world would we go through all of this trouble to talk about our opening play or any play for that matter? Because the devil is in the details. Your goal is to ensure that your client gets from snap to touchdown seamlessly. There is one word in that phrase that is by far the most important— "Touchdown!" If you don't get your client into the endzone, i.e. make a sale, you aren't going to be in business for very long. As we begin evaluating our current process, we must start with the end in mind: we have to make a sale.

First impressions are absolutely everything in sales. It only takes seven seconds to make a first impression, according to a Harvard Business study. In the above example, I went as far as to describe the door kick. Why? Because it makes a first impression, but at a deeper level, those wooden door kicks tend to slide sometimes. What if the door slides as a customer is walking in? Shouldn't we as sales professionals ensure our process is foolproof? Shouldn't we remove every single potential barrier to getting our client into the endzone? If we are quarterbacking the sale, the answer is yes.

Outline every part of your current sales playbook i.e., your process in detail, but once again, do not commentate. Do not write, "Subtle perfume is pumped toward the front door *to make the client feel welcome and set the ambience.*" It doesn't matter what we intend to do. All that matters is what is done and how your client actually interprets it. Do not justify or explain any part of your current process. Simply record your process as if you were a bystander looking in.

How do you pick up the phone? Where do you make calls from? What hours are you available on call? What is the average time within which one can expect a call back? Is that communicated? If so, at which step of your process? Are there any third parties that you'll need to introduce? How are those introductions made and when in the process are they made?

There are thousands of questions we need to be asking ourselves, but the simplest way to ensure we don't miss a single step is to simply go through a sale and record every step along the way. The next time you have a prospect, maybe even this afternoon, pull up your playbook and record the entire process. I recommend that you do this three times with three different clients as it is likely your process will change a little bit since you will be thinking about it every step of the way.

Once you have recorded three sales calls step by step, place each one side by side and outline your current sales playbook. Highlight the steps that most accurately and consistently represent your process.

Record. Record. RECORD!

Outline Current Playbook From Your Client's Perspective

You have now painstakingly outlined every detail of your sales process, but it is through your eyes. It is now time to examine your process through the eyes of your prospective buyer. To do this, you must first select such a prospect.

Selecting the perfect reviewer to give you their opinion of the process is impossible, so we are going to elicit feedback from four reviewers. Two of these reviewers will be prospects you took from snap to touchdown, and then you'll select two reviewers you couldn't get into the endzone. We could select 50 reviewers, but at this point, we are just working to get an understanding of how an outsider views our process.

To approach these candidates for a review, I typically recommend calling up a selected client who got into the endzone and saying something like, "Hey Jack, thanks so much for your business and for choosing me for your _____ needs. I am working on a project to improve my customer experience, and I was wondering if you'd be willing to either schedule a time to sit down or a 15-minute phone call to review your experience. Would you be willing to help me out? I know you probably don't expect it, but I'd also like to give you a $50 gift card for your time and for helping me out. Would scheduling a phone call or a time to sit down work better for you?"

For the clients didn't up in the endzone, I'd recommend a conversation like this: "Good afternoon, Mr. Smith, thanks again for giving me the opportunity to try and earn your business. I'm sorry we weren't able to do business together at this point, but I appreciated your professionalism and noticed you were the sort of guy who paid attention to the details. I was wondering if you'd be able to help me out with a project I am working on to improve our customer experience. It will just take about 15 minutes, is this something you'd be willing to help me out with? I know you probably don't expect it, but I'd also like to give you a $50 gift card for your time and for helping me out. Do you have a moment now or any time available next week for a 15-minute call?"

There will be some people who will flat out refuse to participate, but for the most part, people love helping. They love feeling like their opinion matters. In fact, this is a practice we have started doing with many of our prospects who don't make it into the endzone as a way to re-start the relationship-building and the process. You'll be shocked how surprised your prospects will be that you want their feedback and input!

When you conduct the interview with your four reviewers, do not steer the conversation or ask follow up questions. As salespeople, our MO is to justify our work and process. We always see our process from our perspective, and the goal of this review is to elicit facts and feelings from the customer, based on their experience, that are devoid of your influence. You've had your turn. Now it's your client's turn.

After you have finished all four interviews, combine the two reviewers who became your clients and the two reviewers who did not make it into the endzone. You'll quickly start seeing some correlations and discrepancies. Make note of each of these correlations and discrepancies on your online form, and if the reviewers were extremely off in their evaluation of the process, you may need to consider getting a new batch of reviewers. The goal is to see patterns in your process from your client's perspective. Once you have the combined the feedback of clients and prospects separately, begin looking at those two processes side by side. Many times, the process feels a lot different to the prospects who didn't make it into the endzone than to those who did. Again, when you start seeing patterns in the feedback from the reviewers, you know you are getting good feedback and you can begin analyzing and comparing it to the process you think can take your client down the field.

Where Am I Dropping the Ball?

The hard work is done, so now we get to the part that pays! Go through each part of your process and see where your client is having to take the initiative. Do they have to open the door themselves? Does your client have to call you to schedule a meeting, or do you call them? It is easy to skim over this and write off some of these components as non-important.

Imagine a world in which you as a consumer didn't need to take any initiative. This is the direction our world is headed in, isn't it? More and more devices like Alexis and the Google home order our groceries simply based on what we typically eat, and those groceries are delivered to our doorstep one or two days later. Talk about taking the initiative! Quarterbacking the sale is important because of the joy and ease it brings to your client. But it's also of paramount importance today, because people are becoming accustomed to this concierge level of service that big box retailers have begun offering. In fact, mega companies like Walmart are shifting their marketing strategy to take the initiative for their clients because they are realizing when they sit on the sidelines and expect customers to come to them, they are losing business.

Therefore, this component of analyzing your process and creating your playbook is essential for developing a winning playbook. Do not sit back and justify your process. If you can open the door for your client, then open the door. If your client is reluctant to come to the store, then create an option where they don't have to and the store can reach them. Where else are you dropping the ball?

Shake The Wall

You are putting your effort and energy into creating a process that is tried and tested. You are building a well-oiled machine that predictably produces the best results possible every single time. That's what it means to have a winning playbook.

However, to ensure that the playbook you're creating stands the test of time, you must shake the wall.

With every component of your process, you're laying bricks. You're building a solid brick wall of a process that must stand the test of time. But many people build a process, and then all of a sudden, or slowly over time, the effectiveness of this process diminishes, and clients begin falling through the cracks. Your wall crumbles, and you're left with a bunch of great components of the sales process, but for some reason they're not working together the way you expected them to.

This is why you've got to shake the wall. As you develop your process, put it to the test. Shaking the wall is similar to inviting difficult clients who test the limits of the capability of your process. We briefly discussed this in the chapter on grit, but it's worth mentioning again. Pain and struggles are what shake our walls. This is a good life lesson as well.

My wife and I recently got hooked on Survivor. We have kind of become Survivor geeks, watching past seasons and discussing the game play along the way. If you're not familiar with the game, the concept is to outwit and outlast the other contestants throughout play in the course of 39 days. In order to not get voted out, players must form alliances with other groups of players, so that when there is a vote, they're not on the short end of the stick. The trick is deciphering which alliances are true and which alliances aren't.

There are some players that constitute the Tribal Council, the circle where losing teams vote one of their members off. This in some ways is a good thing. The players that allude to the Tribal Council the longest are never in a position to be voted out. However, a seasoned Survivor player or fan also knows that alluding to the Tribal Council can be very dangerous. Why? Because you've never had an opportunity to shake the wall. Your alliances have not withstood the test of a true vote. You may think that you're on the winning side of an alliance, but until the votes are cast, you don't know who is true and who is merely leading you on. Tribal Councils are a great example of shaking the wall. They bring the truth forth and allow you to see what truly is and is not.

The same is true for our sales process. We can build a beautiful sales processing machine, but if it doesn't stand the test of a

Tribal Council, in other words, if it isn't put to the test, we will not know what works and what doesn't.

Why is this important? When you're building a wall and you have faulty bricks on the third or the fourth row, those faulty bricks might begin to shake or wiggle, and as a result, the entire wall may be compromised. What I do not want you to do is spend hours and days and weeks and months creating a beautiful sales process on paper that hasn't seen any real world application.

So as you begin to implement your playbook, I implore you to not roll it out all at once. If the first step of your playbook is to open the door for your client, then start with implementing the small change of opening the door for your client. After that has been tested and the wall has survived it, it's time to move to the next layer of bricks, or the next step in your sales process. Implementing your playbook should be like building a brick wall. Brick by brick, layer by layer.

It will be incredibly difficult to not roll out your entire playbook. You will want to go all in and make huge changes all at once. But if the first step is opening the door, and you realize a week later that opening the door in fact sets the wrong tone for your sales process, the rest of your process can come crumbling down, and in fact, seem irrelevant. The sales process is a dance where each move and step is interconnected. One move flows into the other. This is both a pro and a con. The pro is that you'll see your client. But the con is that if one part of your dance needs to be changed, there's a good chance other components of your process will also need to be tweaked. Therefore, do not be overzealous in making dozens of changes at one time.

Rather, build the wall, shake the wall, fix the wall, build the wall, shake the wall, fix the wall, build the wall, shake the wall, fix the wall, and so on. You get the point!

Chapter 10

Draft a Winning Team

Quarterbacks are incredible athletes. In high school, they play both sides of the ball, on special teams, and they are the star baseball and basketball players as well. Their pure athleticism is impressive, and they are capable of much more than the average high school athlete.

However, put a quarterback on the field by himself, and he doesn't have a chance of succeeding. He might be fast and have a couple of plays up his sleeve, but when it's one against 11, the 11 will win every single time.

We live in a day and age where autonomy and freedom are the ultimate goals. More entrepreneurs exist today than ever before. The allure of being schedule free and the lack of apparent accountability from people around and above you makes the entrepreneur life desirable.

Just like every great football team, there has never been a successful business with only one person marching down the field. In order to be successful, quarterbacks must have a winning team surrounding them.

Hiring on a Zero-Dollar Budget

We are sales professionals, and we get paid when we sell something. The trick to quarterbacking the sale is we have to deliver an exceptional experience before we get the client into the end zone and get paid. How do we hire a team that can ensure our client gets from snap to touchdown if we don't have deep budgets to draw from?

Barbara Corrcoran, a real estate mogul and a shark on Shark Tank, said that when she began her business, she counted it as a blessing that she didn't have any money. Contrary to what everyone else was doing at the time, she had to think outside the box and find creative solutions that cost a fraction of the price. Mrs. Corrcoran tells her entrepreneur business partners to operate like startups. Figure out how to look like you have a winning team around you, even if you're the only person on the payroll.

You work for a commission check. If someone asked you to serve their client and get paid a commission check to do it, would you gladly help their client? If you make a commission check, then there are other people out there who want to make a commission check too, and they want to work for you and earn your referral. They are, therefore, a zero expense on your payroll.

The teammates you're always going to recruit first and foremost are other third-party commissioned salespeople who get paid to solve the problems your clients have. When you make passes and hand the ball off, you don't have to pay that running back or wide receiver. Your client is paying them, and you are just making the pass or handoff.

Drafting a 100%, third-party commissioned team makes onlookers marvel at the network and sophistication you have, while in reality, all you did was draft the team. They are not on your payroll, and you don't have to contribute to their 401k. You don't have to ask when they're taking vacations or lease an office for them to work out of.

Your clients will be impressed at the ease of doing business with you and by this pack of pros marching them down the field while you sit back and marvel at the team you've put together—without having paid a dime for it.

These players are typically people your client is going to need to interact with during the transaction irrespective. However, when you quarterback the sale, you are making these intentional passes down the field for your client. You are taking the initiative and vetting the thousands of "players" your client would have to pick from in order to draft the best team for them. We have the ability to differentiate ourselves by surrounding ourselves with the best third-party referral sources we know will guarantee a win for our client.

Drafting a winning team doesn't take a big budget: it just takes creativity and a little time in order to draft the best team possible.

Who Do You Draft?

It is easy to overcomplicate this part of building your team, but it doesn't need to be rocket science. Outside of you, who do your clients need to use during your transaction? Make a list, and those are the players we're going to begin drafting!

There are a couple of key players we each need to draft, and they are the players our clients will have the maximum interaction with during a transaction. In insurance, the two most valuable third-party referral partners I need are a restoration company and a body shop. In fact, restoration companies and body shops constitute about 90% of the referrals we make. The same will most likely be true for your transaction. There will be a couple of third parties that your clients will need to use more than any other category. Those key players are going to require the majority of your scouting as you draft your winning team.

In every business, there are also a couple second-tier businesses our clients regularly use. Our clients may need to use glass companies for their windshields or general contractors to do general maintenance for their homes. These second-tier players are equally important to network with, but may not require the same amount of time and energy for vetting as your top-tier referral partners will.

Then there are third-tier "players" our clients will use. For the average sales professional, this tier is completely off their radar. These are the special team players who don't really make big splashes, and if need be, we could still get our clients into the end zone without them. However, a quarterback goes the extra mile, above and beyond what is minimally required.

I love Zig Ziglar's quote: *"There is no traffic on the extra mile."* When we begin drafting third-tier players, we begin to separate ourselves from the pack and provide an exceptional service like no others to our clients.

To illustrate how we can go about drafting a winning team, let's draft a team for a real estate agent who is helping their clients purchase a home.

If you could only draft one player outside of a real estate agent in the real estate transaction, who would it be? The answer is obvious: you need a lender! Almost 99.9% of the time, people cannot purchase a home without financing. The mortgage lender is going to be the first person a buyer goes to before purchasing a home.

The lender, therefore, is the real estate agent's top-tier player. So, if this is the key person for every real estate transaction, why not just draft the best mortgage lender into your team? They work on

100% commission, and I am not aware of any lenders who wouldn't want to be "on your team."

If you're a real estate agent, how many loan officers in town have asked you to send them business? There's not a lack of lenders asking you to throw them a bone. But when you are drafting your winning team, you have a singular objective: find the best lender for your clients.

It is the real estate agent's job to ensure their client gets from snap to touchdown as seamlessly and quickly as possible. The lender is the key player who is going to get that ball most of the way down the field once there's a purchase agreement in hand. Therefore, it's worth every minute of the real estate agent's time to find the best lender for his or her clients.

As a real estate agent begins interviewing job candidates, he will collect names and numbers of the best lenders in town and reach out to each one of them on the phone. Take the call seriously and have several basic questions ready that you'd like to ask your potential teammate. You're looking for aptitude and personality. Do they know what they're talking about and does their personality fit the way you treat your clients? If you're sarcastic and the lender is as dry as a bone, he/she might not be the best fit for you and your clients.

Once you've narrowed your search down to a couple of top lenders, schedule a time to sit down with them and get to know their process and how they do business. Do they quarterback the sale for their clients or do they put the onus of gathering information they could have gathered on their own on their customers? Do they go the extra mile to take the stress off of their clients or are they dead set on hitting their next monthly goal? Do they exhibit the key character traits of a quarterback: grit, leadership, resolve to help their clients win, confidence, humility, initiative, and empathy?

It is the quarterback's job to pick the player they think has what it takes to get the ball into the end zone and provide a consistent experience for their clients. We are not picking the best three options. As sales pros, it is our full-time job to get our clients into the end zone. Therefore, quarterbacks don't pick the best three options and let their clients choose who they'd like to work with. Quarterbacks put in the extra work and put their necks on the line in order to pick the very best third-party player for their clients. Anything less is lazy and unprofessional.

What about recruiting backup players if your top choice for that position is injured (on vacation, sick, etc.)? If you are drafting players who don't have systems in place to ensure every single client that comes to them gets into the end zone, then you've drafted the wrong player. The best lenders always have systems in place to keep business going as usual even when they are out of town, sick, or simply at a golf outing. If the success of that player's business rest solely on his or her back, then you're not in business with another successful quarterback.

I had to learn this early on in my career. I went on vacation for the first time since I had taken on a new lender. I was at the Outer Banks in North Carolina, and after being out at the beach all day, I went back to the beach house to check my emails. I had received an email from that particular lender as well as several missed calls from the client he had sent my way. The client needed an insurance policy before the close of business, and by the time I had checked my email, business was closed.

That lender's client was delayed in closing on their house. Was it my fault? No, but my referral partner passed the ball to me assuming I had what it took to get that ball into the end zone every single time. I didn't. I wasn't a quarterback...yet.

When I got back home, I immediately sat another agent down in my office and devised a system that would ensure this mistake never happened again. That was the beginning of my quarterback journey, and we've been improving the process ever since. Now, I can confidently say that we quarterback the sale every single time, and our business has grown exponentially because of it.

So when you are drafting a winning team, you will never have to draft multiple players for each position. You are only drafting one type of player: other quarterbacks.

Our real estate agent has now drafted his top-tier player. Tier-two players are just as important, but will most likely take less time to recruit. Here are some second-tier players for a real estate agent.

Title Closer

It's easy for sales pros to take the easy option and align themselves with whoever their parent company does business with. Real estate agents are no exceptions. Title companies and real estate brokerages have been in bed with one another for decades, but just because there may be a financial incentive involved doesn't mean it's best for your client to work with your brokerage's title company partnership.

At the end of the day, the choice of the title company and title closer is completely your decision. Buyers don't have any say in the title company. This gives even more importance to your decision. Does the closer look, smell, and carry themselves professionally? Is the title closer neutral or do they bring excitement and energy to the table as your client passes over the end zone line? You've worked too hard getting your client down the field to have a non-descript closing.

This principle applies to all of us. Who is the party involved in getting our clients right over the end zone line? Sometimes, that person is not us. And if we aren't running that ball into the end zone, who is? That player is incredibly important, yet often overlooked.

Home Inspector

The home inspector makes sure the product you're selling is solid. Which player in your sales process inspects your product or service to ensure it is without defect? Is it an underwriter? A quality control firm? A mechanic or engineer? This player may have a small role but provides expert opinions to us and our clients on the product or service we are selling.

Homeowner's Insurance Agent

This responsibility is often passed off to the loan officer in the sales process. There is nothing inherently wrong with the rationale if the real estate agent is throwing the ball to a quarterback loan officer. However, if you toss the ball to your lender and then they pass it to the insurance agent, who gets the glory for pass? The loan officer does! The highlight reel is going to show a trick play where there was a lateral pass to the loan officer who bombed it down the field for a first down! However, if you make that referral to your client, the credit is yours and you further establish yourself as a professional quarterback.

Third-Tier Players

Referring third-tier players is what separates quarterbacks from the rest of their competition. Third-tier players have small roles, but when quarterbacked, take stress off of our clients' plates. For a real estate agent, a homebuyer will need to call their electric company, Charter, ATT, trash guy, and other such services. Will you be able to know personal names of sales reps for your client to call? No, but you can create a cheat sheet including numbers, prompts to push, and recommendations for a quick and easy transition.

For example, DTE Energy is easier to work with over the phone (Insert Phone #), and Consumers Energy is easier to sign up for online (Insert Link). OR – AT&T is faster and $7 cheaper than Consumers in a new neighborhood.

Each player you draft comes with a wealth of professional

knowledge—knowledge that would cost us tens of thousands of dollars to acquire. By spending time drafting the best team for our clients, we are able to create a winning team surrounding us without having to spend a dime. As quarterbacks, the only other players we should draft are quarterbacks. When we draft quarterbacks, we can rest easy knowing that the same experience we brought to the table will be carried on by our referral partners. Our clients will thank us, and our efforts will be multiplied tenfold when we draft a winning team.

ZACH SANTMIER

Part 3

Execution of a Quarterback

Chapter 11

It's Game Day

I get geeky over business plans. There are few things more calming to me than writing down a vision, developing goals, and plotting a course to achieve my dreams.

I had the privilege of speaking at an event where I opened for a successful business coach. The title of his talk was "Developing a Winning Road Map." I got excited, and I rushed through my talk in anticipation of what I was expecting to hear that I knew would surely change my life.

This guy brought it. He spoke for almost four hours about goal-setting, vision-casting, tracking data, and tips and tricks to achieving our dreams. I was excited, because by the end of the seminar, I had written out an incredible business play that led to me making $1,000,000 a month. Not bad for a four hour seminar!

Three weeks later, I hired a business coach for myself. She saw my current business plan and decided I needed a different format. I spent the next four weeks working on my business plan to ensure I had the most realistic and practical way of achieving my dreams.

Ironically, once I had finished my second business plan, they both winded up tacked to my wall, hanging there for me to admire.

This past week, I brought my hammer to work and tore down a wall during business hours. I was sick of looking at those business plans, hoping they'd execute themselves. They were getting me nowhere. They were just plans, but *without a builder, an architect would be out of a job.*

So I tore down a wall that was impeding progress, moved two people into the same office to work with one another, and the plan was converted into action.

Your playbook is useless if you get geeky over drawing up the plays but never get on the field and execute them. We've worked hard to think through your business, evaluate your plays, and develop a process that could replace your client's stress and anxiety with peace and joy.

Saturdays always turn into Sundays. It's game day!

Get The Right Ball

Every Sunday morning, Peyton Manning would go into the locker room with his equipment manager, and in a silent room, he would begin to sort through balls. He'd pick up the first ball, feel it, and if he liked it, toss it to the equipment manager and say, "game." If he didn't like the ball, he'd say, "pre-game."

Weren't the balls all made in the same factory with the exact same material? Why would a professional quarterback waste his time sorting through these seemingly insignificant differences? Peyton Manning knew that every ball was not equal. There were some balls that fit his hand better and made him feel more confident. Not every ball was meant for Peyton.

The same is true for us as sales professionals. We can have a beautiful process that rivals Henry Ford's, but if we are marching the wrong ball down the field, we're going to be set up for failure.

We've all been asked to draw client avatars and get really specific about who we're selling to, but if I'm being honest, those drills have always demotivated me. I don't want to sell insurance only to a 31-year-old woman who wears 37% less makeup than the average woman, is 5'3" and owns a poodle! If that's the only "ball" I am looking to work with, my business is going to go downhill pretty quickly.

On the other hand, I think we've all fallen into the trap of selling to anyone who breathed and had a wallet. This is equally dangerous. You've heard it being said, *"If you stand for anything, you stand for nothing."* The same is true when you are picking your ball. If you are ready to work with any ball, then you can't have a tailored experience that runs smoothly every single time.

Over the past couple of years, I have landed up picking one category of "balls." This has helped me focus on my process and allowed our business to explosively grow thereby work with thousands of new clients.

At Trumble Insurance Agency, our target client is someone in the process of purchasing a home in West Michigan. It's general enough to incorporate over 35,000 people a year within a 50-mile radius, but specific enough to tailor a sales pitch and process aimed directly at them.

The potential of taking on 35,000 new clients a year is exciting, but it's also achievable. If I said I was going to write insurance for every person in West Michigan, the likelihood of me actually achieving that goal is zero. However, with a specific niche that's big enough to get me excited, I can actually have a process that is differentiated in the market place and that sets my business apart and attract those 35,000 clients.

How big does the slice of pie need to be for you to get excited? Would you be motivated to go out and find the three 5-foot-

3-inch tall, poodle-owning ladies I described earlier? If so, then get really specific about who you want to go after and go get them! But if you're like most sales pros, you want a big piece of pie and you want to eat it too! If that's the case, then you need to pick an estimate of people that gets you excited and seems just out of reach. What's the number? Today, my number is 35,000 people a year. In a couple years, that number may not excite me anymore, and I'll need to extend my sphere. The same is true for your business.

What number excites you today that seems just out of reach? What kind of people does your business naturally attract? What are you uniquely good at? Which problems do you or could you solve, which attract the number of people you just decided upon, excite you?

When I put my business through this exercise, I didn't reinvent the wheel. I looked at the business we were producing and I asked myself, "What sort of client seems to have the smoothest experience with our business? If I focused my entire business on that one sort of client, would that excite me?" I quickly realized that we were already doing well helping people purchase insurance during the homebuying process, and once I ran the numbers, 35,000 new clients a year was definitely enough to get me excited!

It's Sunday morning. Become Peyton Manning for a second, and determine the sort of balls you want to take out onto the field. It's game time!

Take The Snap

Getting under center isn't for the faint-hearted. A quarterback gets the play call and then has to put his hands behind a 300lb man, while eleven other mammoths stare him down. In the blink of an eye, the quarterback takes a snap, and reality is brought to bear.

When we take the snap and actually start our sales process, we will quickly find out if our well laid out plan is going to work. Our playbook will be put to the test by external circumstances, a vicious defense that doesn't want us to succeed, and our own limiting beliefs that hold us back.

It's always easier to gain knowledge, make a beautiful plan, and then tack it up on your wall to admire. But our clients need us to start marching down the field. They need us to come into the office with a hammer and tear down the wall!

Let's take action and begin marching our clients down the field. Throw aside the thoughts of insecurity and perfection. Your process won't be perfect, and you may fumble the ball along the way. But we have to take action. We have to take the snap and put our playbook to the test.

Lead the Play

Everything we've worked for will be used when we march down the field. The mindset and playbook of a quarterback collide and are put to the test.

Leading the play takes grit, confidence, a resolve to win, humility, and empathy.

Once you take the snap and the play has begun, everything you believed would happen once the play got under way is put to the test. The pre-snap read is crucial to being proactive, but linebackers and defensive ends will always trying to fake you out. Therefore, while a pre-snap read gives you a head start, it is the post-snap read that executes the play and ensures a victory.

I once had a client who was interested in us putting a home and auto insurance proposal together for her. She was as sweet as could be when I initially met her, so my pre-snap read on her was that she was going to want to chat a bit, have a nice conversation about her new home, and then want to get everything closed on the insurance so she could continue living her "social" life. I took the snap and reality came to bear. I couldn't have been more wrong about this gal.

Once I had put together a preliminary proposal for us to review, we hopped on a call, and immediately I knew my pre-snap reading was way off. This woman wanted to dive deep. She began asking questions about exclusions and wanted to see a full policy form with every single endorsement form that was added on the policy currently as well as all of those that could potentially be purchased. It ended up taking four weeks and around eight hours of my time to go line by line with her as she crossed referenced form after form. She even wanted to amend some of the endorsements on the policy in order to better suit her new home and situation.

I was floored! I wasn't ready for this in my playbook. Sure, I knew the policy language, but I didn't have every policy form at my finger tips to send to her immediately. I had to now execute my post-snap read and dramatically adjust my play to ensure I didn't drop the ball as this play was unfolding at a rapid pace.

Leading the play and executing your playbook isn't going to be perfect every time, but over time, you will get more and more confident under center and as clients call in and you call on prospective clients, your leadership will continue to grow.

Don't stop. Rome wasn't built in a day and leading your playbook can become frustrating, especially as you get started. Your playbook is going to need to be refined and perfected. As you march down the field, you may have to call a couple audibles along the way as you learn your way around the playbook. But don't stop. Keep pushing and keep perfecting. Keep tweaking your playbook as you lead the play down the field until you consistently find yourself and your clients in the endzone every single time!

Chapter 13
Celebrate the Touchdown

One of my favorite things to watch on Sundays are touchdown celebrations. There was definitely a dry spell in the NFL when they banned the celebrations, but they're back, and they're better than ever! Quarterbacks play a role in 95% of all touchdowns. However, the majority of the time, they are not the ones who get the ball over the end zone line. This does not deter their excitement after scoring a touchdown. Quarterbacks celebrate the touchdown without fail.

The goal of the quarterback is to get the ball from snap to touchdown. As we've uncovered throughout this book, quarterbacking the sale requires a well-developed mindset, a willingness to go the extra mile while ensuring the ball is never dropped, and executing the play. We've shed a light on our client's problems and put systems and processes in place to guarantee our client gets their win.

However, I believe that the most underutilized step in our sales process is celebrating the touchdown for our clients.

Humans naturally have two parts of their life when they are profoundly impacted and make lasting memories. When someone experiences deep grief or pain, the memory of it will often last a lifetime. Pain has the ability to change people's outlooks on life, their beliefs, and even how they view themselves. We commemorate these pain points with pomp and circumstance. When there is a death, we spend tens of thousands of dollars on a funeral. Some people get tattoos or purchase expensive keepsakes to remember a sad time in their life. Funerals, tattoos, keepsakes, and the like expand the pain or grief so that when our minds take a snapshot of the moment to store it away as a memory, there is more data, and the event is given greater significance because of its magnification. Whenever we look at pictures of the funeral, glance at the tattoo, or dust the keepsake, we remember that moment of pain, sadness, or grief. Those moments shape us and make us who we are.

However, the same impact can be made when pleasure is experienced. During moments of euphoria, our minds will lock in a snapshot of the experience in the hope that it will never be forgotten. Close your eyes for a moment. What is the first high point you remember in your life? I remember swimming in a pool at an apartment and then, as if it was immediately after, hearing Santa's sleigh bells on Christmas Eve. Later I found out that my parents had given bells to our neighbors who lived above us, producing the sound, but it still didn't diminish the significance of that moment. That memory stuck because the camera lens was open for a long time. Just as with painful events, the longer our minds are exposed to a happy event, the longer that event will be remembered.

During the sales process, we've worked our butts off to make the experience positive, going above and beyond what has been expected of us. Our clients have had an incredible experience. The lens has been opened for a period of time, but it needs to be capped with a moment that will make the rest of the experience memorable. Without a capstone celebration, your sales process will be like a painting that was never outlined. All of the colors and details are there, but the outline is blurry, and the painting will soon be forgotten.

When your client crosses that goal line, and the transaction has been finalized, it's time to celebrate! One of the phrases I've repeated throughout this book is turning stress and anxiety into peace and joy. That's what quarterbacking the sale does, and our clients deserve to remember this positive experience for a lifetime.

Celebrate

This entire process has been about our clients, and the celebration is no different. We are celebrating our clients and what they have accomplished. It's easy to slip into posting how fast you just closed this house on Instagram, but a quarterback shines the light on the client and celebrates all that the client has accomplished to get to this point in their life.

The celebration needs to be memorable. Think back to every birthday party you've had. Which ones do you remember? My guess is you remember one or two where your loved ones went out of their way and did something unexpected or out of the norm. Now try to remember the rest of your birthdays from as far back as you can remember. What did you do on each birthday and who was there? It's hard to recall, isn't it? Our minds don't remember things that are "normal."

One of my favorite examples of this is from a referral partner of mine. This lender, at each closing, gets a basket of custom-made cookies that have the family members' names written on them and then a cookie replica of the home their client just purchased.

It's small, but intentional. As that new home buyer is closing on their purchase, it what is typically a real estate agent heavy transaction, this lender opens up the lenses of time for just a moment so their client remembers them for years to come. The celebration is genuine and memorable. I've chatted with clients months after closing who are still talking about the cookies.

This singular, memorable celebration puts a capstone on the client's experience, and as they cross into the endzone, a positive memory is forever created in their minds.

What could you do to celebrate your client's accomplishment? Maybe start with custom cookies and then move into something more your own. What capstone celebration would make your clients remember their experience with you for a lifetime? What would make *you* remember your experience?

The sales person who celebrates the client is the sales person who is remembered forever. Every other salesman is coloring a picture without outlining the experience. They are soon forgotten as the lines further blur into their distant memories. Our celebration of them doesn't have to be fancy or cost a lot of money. It just has to be memorable, something that sticks out that your client will never forget. Don't skim over the celebration. Opening the lenses of time further solidifies the memory into someone's mind.

We've come this far, it's time to celebrate!

Chapter 14
Do It!

You've made it through the book, and now it's time to do the work. There is a reason why there are very few quarterbacks in America: It's hard work! But hard work first starts with commitment.

Do you believe that giving your client a sales experience that reduces stress and anxiety is a noble goal? Do you believe that your clients deserve an experience where you don't drop the ball? Do you believe your family deserves that you put your best foot forward and bring home as much money as possible? Do you believe that you deserve more? Do you believe that your team deserves a process that is reliable and replicable and that they could take over if you're on vacation or not available at the office?

Think about a world in which you quarterbacked every sale. Your clients stood in the endzone on cloud nine proclaiming, "That was it? That was too easy!" Imagine a life where you knew what you were going to do before you did it. When a client calls in, you have an exact playbook that you've tried and tested. You know that playbook will get them to where they want to go and where you want them to go, leading to a sale. You are no longer shooting from your hip or making up your process as you go. Imagine a customer experience that you or anyone else on your team could step into and win.

What would that do to your life? Would you be able to spend more time with your family? Would you be able to donate more to the charities you care deeply about? Would you be able to spend more time going on the trips you've always dreamed of? How about some more time working on providing even more value in the marketplace? The reason I take quarterbacking so seriously in my organization is because I know that the more we quarterback, the more time we are able to spend producing even more value for our clients. We can grow our business and change our industry! I am able to write this book because we quarterback sales! We have a playbook that is working, and it doesn't need me every second of the day.

There is a lot at stake here, and I am passionate about seeing you succeed in your business and in your life. Now is the time to commit to this quarterback way of life. However, before you commit, I want to lay the groundwork for true commitment.

Commitment means doing what you said you would do despite contrary thoughts, feelings, or emotions. I started this book as a practice in commitment. Books don't write themselves. It takes time to develop them and put words on paper. When we are committed to something, we are saying we will move a mountain with a shovel if that is what is required.

In my family creed, we chant,

> *"I am a winner and a champion. I will move a mountain with a shovel if that's what's required."*

We truly mean this statement. When we say we're going to do something, we do it even if it seems like there is an impassable mountain in front of us. We will do what is required to get the results we desire. As a family, we take commitment seriously.

As you join this family of quarterbacks, you must be aware that we take commitment very seriously. When you begin implementing these lessons, you can't get your foot wet and test the waters. Imagine Tom Brady stepping on the field and telling his team, "I am pretty committed, but before we try and win a football game, I'd first like to just play one snap, and then we'll go ahead from there." His team would have no trust in his authority and wouldn't follow his leadership. The same is true when we begin to quarterback our sales process.

If you start out really strong and quarterback the first play of the sale, your client then expects that same level of service. If you don't continue quarterbacking the sale when your client expects you to take the initiative, you won't and you'll drop the ball. The sale will completely fall apart. In my experience, not quarterbacking the sale at all is more effective than partially quarterbacking the sale.

There's a downside to quarterbacking the sale. Once you begin, your client expects that same level of service and tends to back off and take less and less initiative. You'll find that if you choose to commit to quarterbacking the sale, you'll become known for your initiative and easy process. Your referral partners and clients will sell you to their customers, friends, and family as a salesperson who quarterbacks the entire process, making it easy and stress-free for potential buyers. So once you have dipped your feet in the quarterback waters, there's no way of going back.

So I want to ask you a serious question that I genuinely believe will serve you and has the potential of improving your life: Are you willing to fully commit to being a quarterback?

If your answer is "Yes," then it's time to begin.

You have the tools and you have the knowledge. You are smart enough to read this short book, and you have the guts to make a commitment. The only thing left now is to simply live it. We're here for you and are excited to hear your results as you grow into the quarterback you were created to be. Your clients are going to love you. Best of luck. Let's change the world.

ABOUT THE AUTHOR

Zach Santmier is the Co-Owner and Sales Manager at Trumble Insurance Agency. He, his wife, Lauren, and their two girls live in Grand Rapids, Michigan where both of his insurance offices are located. Zach is passionate about using sales to increase the quality of life for his team and other sales professionals. His Christian faith in Jesus pushes him to be a better husband, father, and business leader.